WRITERS AND THEIR WORK

ISOBEL ARMSTRONG
General Editor

GRACE NICHOLS

GRACE NICHOLS

Sarah Lawson Welsh

NORTHCOTE
BRITISH COUNCIL

First published in 2007 by Northcote House Publishers Ltd, Horndon, Tavistock, Devon, PL19 9NQ, United Kingdom.
Tel: +44 (01822) 810066. Fax: +44 (01822) 810034.

British Library Cataloguing-in-Publication Data
A catalogue record for this book is available from the British Library

ISBN 978-0-7463-1027-4 hardcover
ISBN 978-0-7463-0955-1 paperback

Typeset by TW Typesetting, Plymouth, Devon
Printed and bound in the United Kingdom

To the original Wantage girls: Trudy, Sally, Claire, Heather and Maz – with thanks for three decades of love, friendship and support.

And to the second generation: Harrie-Rae, Ellie, Helena, Martha and, most of all, Imogen. Happy 'small-girl days' to all of you . . .

Contents

Acknowledgements

I am grateful to Professor Isobel Armstrong for giving me the opportunity to write this book on Nichols, to the University of Northampton for granting me generous research leave in order to complete this project and to my former colleagues there for their continued good humour and support. I would also like to thank Grace Nichols for her kind assistance with resources and references. I am only sorry that lack of space ultimately prevented me from including your writing for children in this study, Grace and that this book was completed before *Starting the Flying Fish* (2005) was published. Thanks are due to my former colleagues Ruth Robbins and Simon Perril for their careful reading and helpful comments on the manuscript. Immeasurable thanks to Richard for his wit, his wondrous cooking and all the light, laughter and living he makes possible. (Next time . . .). Finally, I'd like to thank Ella King, a former undergraduate student of mine, for her inspiring dissertation on Caribbean Women's writing and for reminding me why I do what I do.

Parts of this book appeared in an earlier form in the following:

Alison Donnell and Sarah Lawson Welsh (eds), *The Routledge Reader in Caribbean Literature* (London and New York: Routledge, 1996); Sarah Lawson Welsh, 'Critical Myopia and Black British Literature: Reassessing the Literary Contribution of the Post-Windrush generation(s)', *Kunapipi*, 20:1 (1998), 132–42; Sarah Lawson Welsh, '(Un)belonging Citizens, Unmapped Territory: Black Immigration and British Identity in the Post-1945 Period', in Stuart Murray (ed.), *Not On Any Map: Essays on Postcoloniality and Cultural Nationalism* (Exeter: Exeter University Press, 1997), 43–66; Sarah Lawson Welsh, 'The Shape-shifting Fictions of Pauline Melville', in Mary Conde and Thorunn Lonsdale (eds), *Caribbean Women Writers: Fiction in English* (London and Basingstoke: Macmillan, 1999), and Sarah Lawson Welsh, 'The West Indies – 1996', *Journal of Commonwealth Literature*, 32:3, 187–99.

Biographical Outline

1950   Born 18 January in Georgetown, Guyana, the fifth of seven children. Her father was a headmaster. In the same year the first modern political party in Guyana, the People's Progressive Party (PPP), is formed, led by Afro-Guyanese Forbes Burnham with Indo-Guyanese Cheddi Jagan as vice-chairman.

1950–58   Nichols's childhood spent in Stanleyville (also known as Highdam), 'a small country village along the [East] Guyana coast' (HT 296). Nichols's family move to Georgetown, capital of Guyana, when she is 8.

1953   First elections under universal adult suffrage held in Guyana resulting in PPP-led government. Dr Jagan becomes Leader of the House. The constitution is suspended after 135 days and the government dissolved by the British colonial authorities, due to feared 'communist subversion of the government and a dangerous crisis both in public order and economic affairs' (*Guyana: Fraudulent Revolution* (London: Latin America Bureau (Research & Action) Ltd, 1984). British troops are landed in Guyana. Amongst former government members and activists imprisoned by the British authorities was Guyanese poet Martin Carter, who began to write his *Poems of Resistance* whilst in prison. Such events led to Burnham breaking away from the PPP and founding what was to become the People's National Congress (PNC).

1954   Martin Carter's *Poems of Resistance from British Guiana* published.

1954–7   Interim Government Rule in Guyana.

1955   Split in PPP leads to formation of PNC, led by Forbes Burnham.

1957   PPP wins general election and Dr Jagan becomes first premier of British Guiana.

1958   Nichols family move to city, Georgetown. Nichols attends St Stephens Scots School and later the Progressive and Preparatory High School.

1961   PPP wins general election.

1963   Britain agrees to grant British Guiana its independence after another election, in which proportional representation is to be introduced. Eighty-day general strike led by civil service in Guyana, financed by CIA. The locking out of workers by right-wing factions leads to rioting.

1963–4 Civil unrest in Guyana; PNC and United Front (UF) supporters denounce PPP government as communist and tensions erupt into racial violence between mainly African-Caribbean PNC supporters and mainly Indo-Caribbean PPP supporters. Hundreds are killed as riots, violence, arson, murder sweep Georgetown and beyond. Britain refuses to grant British Guiana its independence under PPP rule. Nichols describes these events in *Whole of a Morning Sky*.

1964   Elections under new proportional representation system result in narrow majority for PPP. Governor general of the colony asks PNC to form a coalition government with UF. Forbes Burnham becomes prime minister.

1966   Nichols leaves school aged 16; British Guiana gains its independence from Britain in May and is renamed Guyana.

1967   Nichols graduates with a Diploma in Communications from the University of Guyana; the course involves 'spending some time in the hinterland of our vast and ruggedly beautiful country' (HT 297).

1966–70 Nichols works as a pupil teacher at the Trinity Methodist Primary School.

1968   Introduction of 'overseas vote' effectively massively rigs Guyanese Elections. PNC wins majority and drops UF from coalition.

1970   On 23 February, the anniversary of the Cuffy slave rebellion of 1763, Guyana is declared a 'Co-operative Republic'; a non-executive president replaces governor general. Bauxite industry is nationalised.

1970–76 All major foreign economic assets except banks and insurance companies nationalised.

1972–3 Nichols works as a reporter/feature writer with local newspaper the *Chronicle*.

1973   Clerk with Guyana Telecommunications Ltd. PNC increases its majority in another election.

1973–6 Information assistant with the Government Information Services, Ministry of Information.

1976–7 Freelance journalist in Guyana.

1977   Nichols migrates to Britain with John Agard.

1979   Multiracial independent Marxist party, the Working People's Alliance (WPA) is formed, led by Dr Walter Rodney.

1980   WPA boycott elections. Walter Rodney is assassinated; Burnham agents are believed to have been responsible. Human rights and civil liberties severely affected. Burnham's rule is increasingly autocratic, especially as a new constitution grants him Executive Presidency with extensive powers. *Trust You, Wriggly* is published.

1983   *i is a long memoried woman* published and winner of the Commonwealth Poetry Prize. *Baby Fish and Other Stories* published.

1984   *The Fat Black Woman's Poems* is published.

1985   Runner up for 'The Other Award' for her children's book *Leslyn in London*. Back in Guyana, Forbes Burnham is elected again. He dies later that year and is succeeded by Hugh Desmond Hoyte who reverses many of Burnham's policies.

1986   *Whole of a Morning Sky* and *The Discovery* are published.

1988   *Come On Into My Tropical Garden* and *Black Poetry* are published. Nichols is awarded an Arts Council bursary to work on a new cycle of poems.

1989   *Lazy Thoughts of a Lazy Woman* is published.

1990   *Black Poetry* is reissued as *Poetry Jump-Up*. A drama feature film based on *i is a long memoried woman* and produced by Frances Anne Solomon is awarded the gold medal at the New York International Film and Video Festival. In the UK the BBC broadcasts a full-length drama adaptation of *i is a long memoried woman*.

1991   *No Hickory, No Dickory, No Dock: A Collection of Caribbean Nursery Rhymes* with John Agard, and *Can I Buy a Slice of Sky?: Poems from Black, Asian and Amerindian Cultures* are published.

1992   Cheddi Jagan returns to power after PPP victory in election; Jagan appoints a multiracial cabinet.

1993   *Quartet of Poems* (with Maya Angelou, Alice Walker and Lorna Goodison) is published.

1994   *Give Yourself a Hug* and *A Caribbean Dozen: Poems from Caribbean Poets* (edited with John Agard) are published.

1996   *Sunris* and *Penguin Modern Poets: Jackie Kay, Merle Collins, Grace Nichols*, vol. 8, are published. *Sunris* wins the Guyana Prize for Poetry.

1997   *We Couldn't Provide Fish Thumbs* and *Asana and the Animals* are published.

1999–   Nichols becomes first writer in residence at the Tate
2000   Gallery, London, working with schools on poems inspired by paintings in the collection.

2000   *The Poet-Cat* is published.

2001   Nichols wins the Cholmondeley Award.

2004   *Number Parade* (with Jackie Kay, John Agard, Nick Toczek and Mike Rosen) is published.

2004   *Paint Me a Poem* and *From Mouth to Mouth* (edited with John Agard) are published.

2005   *Starting the Flying Fish* is published.

2006   *Everybody Got a Gift* is published.

Abbreviations and References

The following abbreviations refer to works by Grace Nichols

FBW   *The Fat Black Woman's Poems* (London: Virago, 1984)

HT   'Home Truths', in E. A. Markham (ed.), *Hinterland: Caribbean Poetry from the West Indies and Britain* (Newcastle-upon-Tyne: Bloodaxe, 1989), 296–8

ILMW   *i is a long memoried woman* (London: Karnak House, 1983)

LTLW   *Lazy Thoughts of a Lazy Woman* (London: Virago, 1989)

PGN   *The Poetry of Grace Nichols*, programme 3 in the *Poetry Backpack* series for schools, BBC television, 1997

R3F   Radio 3 Feature, dramatization of *i is a long memoried woman* for the BBC

S   *Sunris* (London: Virago, 1996)

WMS   *Whole of a Morning Sky* (London: Virago, 1986)

The following refer to other key works

AB   Avtar Brah, *Cartographies of Diaspora: Contesting Identities* (London and New York: Routledge, 1996)

AL   Audre Lorde, *Sister Outsider: Essays and Speeches* (Freedom, CA: Crossing Press, 1984)

AO   Alicia Ostriker, *Stealing the Language: The Emergence of Women's Poetry in America* (London: Womens Press, 1986)

B&T   Diana Brydon and Helen Tiffin, *Decolonising Fictions* (Sydney, Mundelstrup and Hebden Bridge: Dangaroo Press, 1993)

BD&S   Beverley Bryan, Stella Dadzie, and Suzanne Scafe, *The Heart of the Race: Black Women's Lives in Britain* (London: Virago, 1985)

C&L   Mary Conde and Thorunn Lonsdale (eds), *Caribbean Women Writers: Fiction in English* (London: Macmillan, 1999)

D&LW   Alison Donnell and Sarah Lawson Welsh (eds), *The Routledge Reader in Caribbean Literature* (London and New York: Routledge, 1996)

EO   Evelyn O'Callaghan, *Woman Version: Theoretical Approaches to West Indian Fiction by Women* (London: Macmillan, 1993)

GG   Gabriele Griffin, 'Writing the Body: Reading Joan Riley, Grace Nichols and Ntozake Shange', in Gina Wisker (ed.), *Black Women's Writing* (Basingstoke: Macmillan Press, 1993), 19–42

GWW   Gina Wisker, 'Weaving Our Own Web: Demythologising/Remythologising in the Work of Contemporary Women Writers', in Gina Wisker (ed.), *It's My Party: Reading Twentieth Century Women's Writing* (London: Pluto Press, 1994), 104–28

GWI   Gudrun Webhofer, *'Identity' in the Poetry of Grace Nichols and Lorna Goodison* (Lewiston, NY: Edwin Mellen Press, 1996)

HC   Hélène Cixous, 'The Laugh of the Medusa', in Dennis Walder (ed.), *Literature in the Modern World* (Oxford: Oxford University Press, 1990), 316–25

JB1   James Berry (ed.), Introduction, *Bluefoot Traveller* (London: Limehouse Publications, 1976)

JB2   James Berry (ed.), Introduction to 2nd edition of *Bluefoot Traveller* (Walton-on-Thames: Thomas Nelson and Sons, 1981)

JG   Jana Gohrisch, 'Gender and Hybridity in Contemporary Caribbean Poetry', in *Anglistentag 1997 Giessen: Proceeedings*, ed. Raimund Borgmeier, Herbert Grabes and Andreas H. Jucker (Trier: WVT, 1998), 139–56

JM   John McLeod, *Beginning Postcolonialism* (Manchester and New York: Manchester University Press, 2000)

JP   James Procter (ed.), *Writing Black Britain 1948–1998* (Manchester University Press: 2000)

KD   Kwame Dawes (ed.), *Talk Yuh Talk: Interviews with Anglophone Caribbean Poets* (Charlottesville and London: University Press of Virginia, 2001)

LN   Lauretta Ngcobo (ed.), *Let It Be Told: Black Women Writers in Britain* (London: Virago, 1988)

MB   Maggie Butcher, 'In Conversation with Grace Nichols', *Wasafiri*, 8 (1988), 17–20

PB   Paula Burnett, 'Epic, a Woman's Place: A Study of Derek Walcott's *Omeros* and Jean Binta Breeze's "A River Called Wise"', in Vicki Bertram (ed.), *Kicking Daffodils* (Edinburgh: Edinburgh University Press, 1997), 140–52

PP   Paraskevi Papaleonida, '"Holding my beads in my hand": Dialogue, Synthesis and Power in the Poetry of Jackie Kay and Grace Nichols', in Vicki Bertram (ed.), *Kicking Daffodils* (Edinburgh: Edinburgh University Press, 1997), 125–39

SC   Selwyn Cudjoe (ed.), *Caribbean Women Writers: Essays from the First International Conference* (Wellesley, MA: Calaloux, 1990)

SN   Susheila Nasta, 'Beyond the Millennium: Black Women's Writing', *Women: A Cultural Review*, 11:1/2 (2000), 71–6

WH   *Woman's Hour* interview with Grace Nichols, BBC Radio 4, 1997

1

Charting the Terrain

BLACK BRITISH WOMEN'S WRITING: A CASE OF CRITICAL NEGLECT

In comparison with many of the writers featured in this series, the work of Guyanese-born Grace Nichols remains relatively unknown to general readers. This is despite a generous output of one novel, four major poetry collections and over fourteen books for children, as well as frequent inclusions in anthologies since Nichols came to Britain in 1977.[1] In the 1990s, Nichols was a recommended writer for the National Curriculum syllabus for English in Britain and her writing is frequently taught at degree level in British universities and colleges of higher education, although still frequently only on courses on women's writing, postcolonial or 'new' literatures in English. Very little critical comment on Nichols's work exists. That which can be found is concentrated overwhelmingly in collections of critical essays on Caribbean women's writing such as Selwyn Cudjoe's *Caribbean Women Writers* (1990) or on black women's writing[2] or in specialist postcolonial literature journals such as *Wasafiri* and contemporary poetry journals such as *Poetry Review*. The paucity of critical materials on Nichols may be in part due to the relatively small number of published interviews and commentaries on her work given by the author herself, but it is also, crucially, part of a wider critical neglect of black British – and particularly black British women's – writing historically, which I have termed elsewhere a 'selective amnesia' or 'critical myopia' on the part of readers and critics.[3] More recently, Susheila Nasta has similarly commented:

1

The history of [black women's writing in Britain] raises several controversial questions. It is not a question of volume or quality, of whether any is being written, but one of visibility: whether or not the voices of these writers are heard, listened to and echoed back into a mythic consciousness. This, as we all know, is obviously linked to the cultural politics which surrounds them. I say 'surrounds' because, from the outset, writing by African, Caribbean, Asian and Black British women has been (when viewed from the outside as it usually is) pocketed, ghettoised. (SN 71, 73)

Nasta contrasts the profile and 'positioning of black women's writing in Britain today' to the situation in North America:

Unlike in the United States, where figures such as the Nobel-winning Toni Morrison or the Poet Laureate Maya Angelou are highly acclaimed literary figures, literary voices by black women in Britain seldom attract any serious critical or indeed scholarly attention. Nor do such writers have rooms in academic institutions ... very few of these writers are featured in the curricula of academic institutions in any permeated sense – although they might be taught together as an option on 'black women's writing,' though even this in my experience has been very limited as 'black women's writing' usually refers to the work of African-Americans ... There remain far too few female academics of colour in this country who might attempt to prioritize some of these writings ... far too few black literary agents and literary editors or journalists on the 'influential' critical pages ... (SN 72–3)

The publication in 1991 of *Motherlands*, a collection of critical essays on Black Women's writing from Africa, the Caribbean and South Asia, edited by Susheila Nasta was prompted by Nasta's view that 'there is, in this country, an utter lack of *visible*, home-grown black women's writing' [my emphasis] (SN 73) and a serious critical neglect of black women's writing, despite the appearance of a plethora of anthologies of such writing in the 1980s and early 1990s.[4] *Motherlands* was written in an attempt to redress this imbalance. Significantly, in Nasta's view, little has changed and 'there remains now [in 2000] as then [1991] very little serious scholarly investigation of these works' (SN 73). She notes the absence of a full-length study of black women's writing in Britain and the continuing problem of it frequently being read alongside African-American women's writing, or through creative and critical paradigms derived from it, an essentializing, universalizing move which implies that black women's writing is a homogenous category.

HISTORICIZING BLACK BRITISH WRITING

Nasta's words echo those of Jamaican-born poet and critic James Berry in his 1976 introduction to *Bluefoot Traveller*, one of the first collections of black British writing to be published in Britain. Berry complained that: 'Westindians here are a long way away from the dynamic cultural activities of American blacks or their fellow Westindians at home. They are grossly underexplored, underexpressed, underproduced and under-contributing' (JB1 9).

His comments reflected a profound sense of the 1970s as a transitional period in black British culture. The 1950s and 1960s had witnessed an explosion in West Indian – especially prose fictional – writing, much of it produced by West Indians who had come to Britain in search of jobs and better publishing prospects (e.g. Sam Selvon, George Lamming) or to attend British universities (e.g. Kamau Brathwaite, V. S. Naipaul). Writers such as Sam Selvon and V. S. Naipaul from Trinidad, George Lamming from Barbados, Wilson Harris, Edgar Mittleholzer and Jan Carew from what was then British Guiana (now Guyana) and Andrew Salkey and John Figueroa from Jamaica, found a particularly fruitful outlet for their early work in the BBC radio programme *Caribbean Voices*, produced by Henry Swanzy and broadcast live from London to the Caribbean between 1945 and 1951. *Caribbean Voices* facilitated exchanges between Britain and the Caribbean, and perhaps more importantly between writers from different islands and territories, as well as forging a sense of common 'West Indian' literary endeavour. As Lamming has suggested 'no islander from the West Indies sees himself as a West Indian until he encounters another islander in foreign territory . In this sense, most West Indians of my generation were born in England.'[5]

Between 1948 and 1958 alone approximately one hundred novels by Caribbean writers were published in Britain. The 1950s have therefore commonly been referred to as 'boom

3

years' for West Indian literature, despite the ex/centric location of much of this publishing activity outside of the Caribbean. The key figures in this literary efflorescence have
likewise been regarded as pioneers. That such an overwhelmingly male-authored body of writing has been, until very
recently, much better represented in both critical studies of
Caribbean literature and on university courses than women's
writing from black Britain and the Caribbean, is no coincidence, for these were the writers and texts which went on to
form an emergent West Indian literary canon.

Interestingly, this 'generation' of West Indian writers basing
themselves in London in the 1950s and 1960s have also been
seen as the first of a succession of generations of writers of
Caribbean origin in Britain.[6] Nichols, when asked if she has
tried to understand herself through this generational framework, comments:

> I don't know if I have ... but I do feel part of it in the sense that
> you do feel a sense of tradition and continuation ... [even though]
> the whole tradition of Caribbean writing is still fairly new, still
> fairly young ... When I look back, we didn't study any of our
> writers in school when I was ... a young child.[7] [Kamau]
> Brathwaite and [Derek] Walcott probably were then making their
> presence felt on the whole literary scene, so we haven't had a long
> tradition. And to create you need that whole climate around you
> in which you can feel empowered and ... a sense of freedom
> which women haven't had in the Caribbean. (KD 141–3)

As a number of Caribbean islands and territories, including
Jamaica, Trinidad and Guyana, gained their independence
from the British colonial authorities in the early and mid 1960s,
there were hopes that the intensification of cultural activity
and debate occurring in the Caribbean might also be realized
amongst West Indian artists in Britain. Certainly by the 1960s
a number of developments signalled optimistic movements
towards consolidating a black artistic community in Britain. In
1966, two West Indians in Britain, Trinidadian journalist and
publisher John La Rose and Barbadian poet and historian,
Kamau Brathwaite founded CAM, the Caribbean Artists'
Movement. Over the course of the decade CAM would provide
a vital forum of critical and cultural exchange for West Indian

4

writers and artists in Britain much as *Caribbean Voices* had done for Caribbean writers in Britain in the 1950s. However, by the early 1970s CAM had folded and *Savacou*, the CAM journal launched in 1969, was being produced and edited by Brathwaite in Jamaica rather than in Britain.[8]

Nichols arrived in Britain with her partner, fellow Guyanese poet John Agard, in 1977, the year after Berry complained of the absence in Britain of the kind of 'dynamic cultural activities of American blacks or their fellow Westindians at home' (JB1 9). Although she had already begun to write in Guyana, having completed a few chapters of the novel which was to become *Whole of a Morning Sky*, and produced a number of poems and short stories there, most of her writing has been undertaken in Britain. Nonetheless, Nichols can be seen as one of new generation of literary voices from the Caribbean whose work reflects wider changes taking place there in the 1970s. Exciting new developments were taking in two main areas: the number of writers (especially poets) making use of grassroots, indigenous cultural forms and using creole or nation language[9] in their work, and the increased publication of women's writing.

In 1976 Berry could only see these creative developments in stark contrast to the climate of disappointment, indirection, even despair, registered by those like himself who remained in Britain and who continued to seek to encourage black British creativity. Indeed, the 1970s in Britain are often remembered only negatively as a decade marked by continued racism, exclusion and increased hostility towards Britain's black population. However, these were also to be significant years for black and feminist activism. It is no coincidence that the singular black British poetic voice of the 1970s, that of Linton Kwesi Johnson, emerged through this activist route and his earliest work developed out of poetry workshops which he and others organized within the Black Panther movement. The subjects of Johnson's highly politicized poetry, as well as his striking use of creole or 'nation language' and unique performance style quickly ensured him a high profile. This was confirmed when in 1975, the Arts Council sponsored the making of a BBC documentary about him: *Dread Beat An' Blood*.

Not only did Johnson's poetry present a coruscating challenge to the manifold exclusions and racisms of British society, but his vision for Britain's black and working-class populations was a thoroughly radicalizing one, grounded in demotic language and community action. In both respects, his poetry was to clear the way for a new generation of black British poets in the 1980s, who would continue to address these subjects and to explore the use of nation language in their work. Certainly some of Nichols's British-based poems such as the 'In Spite of Ourselves' section in *The Fat Black Woman's Poems* properly belong to this tradition of black British writing and, although in their use of creole or nation language Johnson and Nichols share an indebtedness to ground-breaking Caribbean literary figures such as Jamaican poet Louise Bennett, Nichols is at least partly indebted to Johnson for pioneering its use in a black British context.

Groups such as the Brixton Black Women's Group (BBWG) and the nationally based Organisation of Women of Asian and African Descent (OWAAD) were also founded in the 1970s (in 1973 and 1978 respectively) and began to campaign against racism and sexism within a range of contexts. Crucially, such organized frameworks for black women (and women more generally) to associate were to nurture a number of writers and make possible some of the most important and promising publications by black women in the early 1980s such as Barbara Burford's *A Dangerous Knowing* (1985) and Beverley Bryan, Stella Dadzie and Suzanne Scafe's *The Heart of the Race* (1985). Susheila Nasta goes as far as to argue that writing by black women in Britain

> has traditionally existed outside the academy . . . in the world of community writing workshops, performance arts and organized groups such as the Asian Woman writers alliance . . . They exist, in my opinion, healthily, outside their 'posts' and have not yet been labelled or categorized further than their ethnicity. This is surprising in a literary climate which . . . has fetishized alterity and the idea of the Other. (SN 72)

She recognizes the positive, subversive potential of this positioning: 'Perhaps as Carole Boyce Davies suggests, it is precisely because this varied body of writing and the multiple sites from which it has evolved have remained outside the institutional and the canonical that we can see these works as what she calls "uprising textualities"' (SN 73).

However, Nasta is also mindful of the damaging consequences of the relative 'invisibility' of black women's writing in Britain outside such specialized circles, citing the example of the huge media coverage given to British Asian comedian Meera Syal's first novel, *Anita and Me* (1996), because of her film and television profile in Britain, whilst 'at least ten earlier Bildungsroman testimonies by writers of the Asian Women's Writers Collective' (SN 74) went unnoticed.

Overall, the 1970s were to be absolutely crucial in bringing to the fore a new generation of literary voices and laying the foundations for the creation of a new literary aesthetic which could be termed 'black British' rather than West Indian or West Indian-British. Arriving in Britain in 1977 and starting to publish in the early 1980s, Nichols was to be part of this new generation of writers. By 1981, Berry was able to write in his introduction to the revised edition of *Bluefoot Traveller*: 'Since the first *Bluefoot Traveller* appeared in 1976, new developments have called for a fresh selection of poems. Britain's Caribbean community . . . involves itself much more intensely in expressing its cultural background. It has become more active in writing and publishing and in the opening of local bookshops' (JB2 6). He was also pleased to be able to note that 'In the original anthology there were no women contributors. Suitable work from women writers had not been submitted or found. That situation has changed here' (JB2 6).[10]

Indeed, Berry's new optimism was prescient as the 1980s and 1990s in Britain were noteworthy for the publication of a number of new West Indian and black British writers, and for the appearance of a significant number of anthologies wholly or partly dedicated to West Indian and black British writing. Early black British writing was anthologized in *Black British Writers in Britain: 1760–1890* (1991), edited by Paul Edwards and David Dabydeen, whilst contemporary black writing in Britain was first anthologised in two editions of James Berry's *Bluefoot Traveller* (1976 and 1981). Berry's next anthology, the influential *News for Babylon – The Chatto Book of Westindian-British Poetry* (1984), was the first to include Nichols's work although his choice of poets was still overwhelmingly male-dominated. It was swiftly followed by *A Dangerous Knowing: Four Black Women Poets* (1985), edited by Barbara Burford. The

7

latter was a ground-breaking publication in many respects: not only did it give more substantial space to Nichols's work and that of the other three poets, Barbara Burford, Jackie Kay and Gabriela Pearse, but it was resolutely committed to opening up publishing to the kind of 'difference, diversity and unpredictability' (Nichols, LN 98) which Nichols herself has declared 'make [her] tick'. The incisive introduction and Burford's role as a forceful spokesperson for some of the issues faced by these and other black writers in Britain make it an important cultural document as well as an important early collection of creative writing.

This might equally be said of *The Heart of the Race*, a wide-ranging account of *Black Women's Lives in Britain* by Beverley Bryan, Stella Dadzie and Suzanne Scafe, which appeared in the same year (1985). Like Burford, its three authors came from backgrounds of activism in 'Black, community and women's politics' (LN 121), including the Brixton Black Women's Group (BBWG) and the nationally based Organisation of Women of Asian and African Descent (OWAAD). They chose to write the book as a collective, convinced that 'it was high time we started to record our version of events, from where we stood as Black women in Britain in the 1980s' (BD&S 1). As they noted in their introduction to *Heart of the Race*:

> Over the past ten years, we have seen the appearance of volumes of material documenting our struggles as Black people, and . . . we welcomed this for we had relied for too long on the version of our story put forward by white historians and sociologists . . . we had seen the women's movement follow suit, documenting 'herstory' from every angle except our own. But, despite the efforts of Black men and white women to ensure that we were no longer 'hidden from history', there was still a gaping silence from Black women. Thanks to our sisters in the United States, this silence is at last beginning to be broken, and for the first time Black women have a voice. But that voice comes from America, and although it speaks directly to our experience in Britain, it does not speak directly of it.   (BD&S 1)

Lauretta Ngcobo's *Let It Be Told: Black Women in Britain*, published two years later in 1987, spoke 'directly of' this experience by focusing on ten black women writers in Britain, including Nichols, and letting the writers themselves speak about their writing practices, their experiences and how the frequently exclusionary politics of publishing and other issues impacted upon their lives. Nichols was also included in three further anthologies of women's writing in the 1980s: *Ain't I A Woman!: Poems by Black and White Women* (1987), edited by Illona Linthwaite, *Watchers and Seekers: Creative Writing by Black Women in Britain* (1987), edited by Rhonda Cobham and Merle Collins and *Charting the Journey: Writings by Black and Third World Women* (1988), edited by S. Grewal, L. Landor and P. Parmer.

Despite having lived in Britain for a decade, Nichols continued to be categorized as a Caribbean writer in this period, as the inclusion of her work in collections such as *The Penguin Book of Caribbean Verse in English* (1986), edited by Paula Burnett, *Hinterland: Caribbean Poetry from the West Indies and Britain* (1989), edited by E. A. Markham, *Voiceprint: An Anthology of Oral and Related Poetry from the Caribbean* (1989), edited by Stewart Brown, Mervyn Morris and Gordon Rohlehr, and *Her True-True Name: An Anthology of Women's Writing from the Caribbean* (1989), edited by Pamela Mordecai and Betty Wilson, testifies. However, the problematic matter of categorizing Nichols and other black writers of Caribbean origin in Britain clearly continued to interest or unsettle a number of critics and interviewers. Having been excluded from *The Penguin Book of Contemporary British Poetry*, edited by Blake Morrison and Andrew Motion in 1982, West Indian and black British poets gradually found themselves admitted to the pages of a range of anthologies in the 1980s, from a single poem in *The Faber Book of Political Verse* (1986), edited by Tom Paulin,[11] to the rather more generous selection in *Angels of Fire – An Anthology of Radical Poetry in the '80s* (1986), edited by Sylvia Paskin et al. Nichols's work was also included in *Grandchildren of Albion: Voices and Visions of Younger Poets in Britain* (1992), edited by Michael Horovitz, and the tellingly titled *So Very English* (1991), edited by Marsha Rowe. Most interesting of all was the placing of black British poets in a section of their own, alongside three other sections in *The New British Poetry* anthology (1988), edited by Gillian Allnutt, Fred D'Aguiar, Ken Edwards and Eric Mottram.

By the early 1990s Nichols's work was appearing in a wide range of anthologies, including *Six Woman Poets* (1992), edited by Judith Kinsman and *Sixty Woman Poets* (1993), edited by Linda France, as well as in journals and magazines. However, the 1990s in Britain were strangely schizophrenic years for black writers in Britain as they simultaneously experienced increased media interest in themselves, such as that generated by the publication of Victor Headley's London-based novel *Yardie* in 1992 or the fiftieth anniversary of Windrush celebrations,[12] and serious critical neglect of their actual writing. It is fair to say that if Berry's 'anxieties on the creative front were to be largely allayed by the tremendous energy, diversity and quality of Black British writing produced in the next decade, those on the critical front were not. Whereas the cultural politics of feminist approaches to Caribbean women's writing and theories of post-colonial literature were to be articulated and interrogated with increasing sophistication in the 1980s and 1990s, a specific and cognate critical attention to black British *literature* (as opposed to Black British cultural praxis more generally) would continue to be neglected' (D&LW 297).

As recently as 1996 Linton Kwesi Johnson commented on the regrettable lack of a critical tradition for black British writers like himself: 'In terms of my own work, I could have benefited from a critical tradition. We didn't have one at that time and we're only beginning to scratch at one in this country now'.[13] Susheila Nasta has called for 'an attempt to move beyond what I call 'apprenticeship criticism' in terms of black women's writing in this country, pieces which celebrate the new voices of black writers, their startling experimentation with language and so on and [the need to] attempt to consolidate and excavate more fully' (SN 75). Crucially, this means historicizing black British writing and within cultural criticism 'evol[ving] . . . a critical commentary on the poetics of black literature as well as the arts and film' (SN 75). Recent publications such as James Procter's *Writing Black Britain 1948–1998* (2000), *Black British Culture and Society* (1999), edited by Kwesi Owusu, and *An Introduction to Black British Culture* (2001), edited by Alison Donnell have already started to establish the foundations for this project.

One problem, as James Procter notes in his general introduction to *Writing Black Britain 1948–1998*, has been the tendency for anthologies of black writing in Britain from Berry's 1976 *Bluefoot Traveller* onwards to be 'characterised by their immediacy, or "nowness": there is no historical conception of a discourse within these anthologies, which tend to present a round-up of writings available "there and then"'. He suggests that

> on the one hand this reflects and reproduces a more pervasive 'forgetfulness' within the field. On the other hand, it is perhaps symptomatic of a publishing industry that is reluctant to commit itself financially to a more ambitious, costly, historical anthology of black British writing ... Such publishing houses, whilst helping to disseminate black writings in Britain, have also assisted in de-historicizing that literature [by] confining it to the present. (JP 8–9)

The cultural and political urgency of placing black British writers in more informed contexts and of reassessing the contribution of West Indian and black British writers to literature in English has arguably never been greater.

'A WRITER ACROSS TWO WORLDS' OR BORDER CROSSINGS

This study of Nichols will therefore place her work within a specifically Caribbean *and* a diasporic black British context. Nichols herself has tended to privilege a Caribbean or Guyanese identity. For example, when asked in 1988 whether she saw herself 'as a Guyanese poet living and working in Britain, or as contributing to and as part of a new tradition in British literature, a Black British tradition', Nichols replied:

> Yes, to some extent; but largely I think I see myself as a Caribbean poet, I like to think of myself as a Caribbean person because the Caribbean embraces so much ... You have Africa, you have Asia and Asian culture, you have European culture, and the Amerindian, the indigenous culture. It's all there. So I prefer to use the word Caribbean, though in a different context I might say ... I'm a Guyanese writer. (MB 18)[14]

More recently, she has spoken of

11

an inner need in me to recreate and celebrate all that is mine and that means the Caribbean and British culture. Because people often put you into little boxes and at times they almost want you to make a choice . . . I suppose I am a writer across two worlds, I just can't forget my Caribbean culture and past, so there's this constant interaction between the two worlds: Britain and the Caribbean. (*PGN*)

Rather than seeing Nichols's 'Caribbeanness' and 'Britishness' as dual affiliations simplistically opposed, I will therefore argue that Nichols's work is one of constant border crossings in which a continuum of cultures, times, psychic and territorial spaces are creatively explored.[15] This is particularly relevant to the third, fourth and final chapter in which the notion of journeying, migration and border crossing is explored most fully.

However, some important qualifications need to be made. The fact that Nichols is both a thoroughly Caribbean poet and a black British poet, a writer seemingly at ease within several cultural traditions and linguistic forms, is often cited approvingly by publishers, critics and teachers, as if such impeccable multicultural credentials are all that is needed to render her work rewarding to read and fascinating to study. The dangers in such enthusiastic but relatively superficial appraisals of Nichols's work, are twofold: firstly, that her more accessible and apparently 'light-hearted' work is elevated over that which fits less comfortably into readers' conscious or unconscious expectations of Nichols as the purveyor of humorous poems and colourful Caribbean 'exotica', or secondly, that her more radical and challenging poems are seen only as the logical extension of her apparent role as a spokesperson for 'oppressed' black women in Britain: 'a little black blood/ undressed/ and validation/ for the abused stereotype/ already in their heads', as Nichols herself terms it in 'Of Course When They Ask for the "Realities" of Black Women' (*LTLW* 52).

The concept of 'border crossing' also needs to be carefully glossed, derived as it is from a more interdisciplinary body of scholarship on 'border theory' and used in a variety of theoretical contexts – feminist, lesbian and gay, postcolonial, postmodern – which are not always cognate. Avtar Brah defines borders as 'arbitrary dividing lines that are simultaneously social, cultural and psychic'.[16] Not only are borders literally 'territories to be patrolled against those [who are constructed] as outsiders, aliens ... Others', but the border can be seen 'as a metaphor for psychological, sexual, spiritual, cultural, class and racialised boundaries'. The concept of the border can thus be mobilized to speak of 'social relations, the everyday lived experience, and subjectivity/identity' (AB 198). To cross borders is thus to move 'across shifting cultural, religious and linguistic boundaries ... [to] journey across geographical and psychic borders' and, as a number of feminist critics have argued, to conceive of one's self as being simultaneously 'situated within gendered spaces of class, racism, ethnicity, sexuality, age' (AB 204).

This study shows how Nichols's work combines border crossings of both kinds. The poems discussed in the third, fourth and final chapters chart and explore the legacies of pain, separation and loss which, historically at least, have accompanied the geographical and psychic journeys of the African slave and the twentieth-century Caribbean migrant, whilst those in chapter 2 examine the 'dominantly construed and ever shifting boundaries of gender and [race]'[17] which are part of the 'everyday, lived experience' of being a black woman in Britain. However, the study also demonstrates how in practice the two kinds of border crossing are never as discrete. Indeed, it argues that Nichols's writing is characterized by exactly this kind of collapsing of binaries, the intermingling and overlap which is characteristic of cultural hybridity, one of the focuses of the final chapter.

Whether the term 'border crossing' or my preferred terms, 'discrepant cosmopolitanisms'[18] and 'discordant belongings',[19] are used to describe Nichols's mapping of a more complex sense of 'unbelonging' as well as belonging in her work and her complex location as a Caribbean and a black British writer, what seems less contested is that she is one of the most exciting and challenging poets and writers of our time.

Ultimately, Nichols's is a poetry which recognizes that 'diasporas are also potentially the sites of hope and new beginnings' (AB 193). Nichols's major female poetic personae in *i is a long memoried woman*, *Starting the Flying Fish* and the title poem of *Sunris*, 'journey towards self-discovery and self-naming' (*S* 4) by first reclaiming or reappropriating aspects of their (African and Caribbean) heritage, their ancestry, history, mythology and culture, what Nichols terms 'all my lives/ strung out like beads' (*ILMW* 86). However, in these and many of her other poems the ultimate power lies in the present and in the potential of the self to heal and to grow: 'the power to be what I am/ a woman/ charting my own futures/ a woman/ holding my beads in my hand' (*ILMW* 86).

NATION LANGUAGE

> We speak creole, we need creole, we cannot function without creole, for our deepest thought processes are bound up in the structure of creole, but we hold creole in contempt.
>
> – Merle Hodge, 'Challenges of the Struggle
> for Sovereignty'[20]

> Language is the only homeland.
>
> – Czeslaw Milosz, quoted by Paule Marshall in
> 'The Making of a Writer: From the Poets in the Kitchen'[21]

One crucial context for an understanding of Nichols's work is that of 'nation language' or creole. Creole is often erroneously called 'dialect' or patwa and regarded as a broken and degenerate tongue which is inferior to standard English. In fact, creoles are recognized linguistic forms which are found the world over. They develop from quite specific conditions of contact between different language groups, such as that between African slaves of different tribes and their European masters, where establishing a common medium of communication or *lingua franca* is imperative. Given the right conditions, this first contact language may develop into a more stable and complex pidgin, and finally, over a period of time, into an even more sophisticated creole or 'nation language'. Whereas a pidgin is usually not the first language of a given speech community, a creole may be. In the Anglophone (English-speaking Caribbean) creoles are usually comprised of a largely European derived lexicon (or vocabulary) and an African syntax or grammatical base. The African influence can be seen in formations such as 'tall-tall' or 'dou-dou' in order to signify magnitude, intensity or degree as well as in particular items of vocabulary.[22] These include 'pickney' (meaning child) or 'nyam' (meaning eat), which clearly derive from non-European sources.

The type and amount of creole spoken by an individual speaker within a given language community, depends on a number of factors including the speaker's geographical location, educational background and social status. Linguists agree that most speakers exhibit a linguistic competence, or ability to speak a range of creole along a section of what they call the 'creole continuum'. The creole continuum is a linguistic model which plots different forms within a single creole from the broadest (*basilectal*) varieties at one end of the spectrum, through *mesolectal* varieties in the middle, to those which most closely resemble standard English at the other end (*acrolectal* varieties). Crucially, the model of the creole continuum is not a fixed but a dynamic one, allowing for linguistic change and development at both ends of the continuum, as for example standard English is affected by creole forms or vice versa.

The specific history of creoles in the Caribbean is very important. Indeed, one of the most important poets of the region, Kamau Brathwaite, has coined the phrase 'nation language' to suggest the foundational role of creole language in defining a people or nation. It is also a more positive, affirmative term than 'dialect' or 'patwa' (from the French *patois*), terms which still retain the derogatory suggestion that creole is not properly a real or fully developed language.

In his 'electronic lecture' *History of the Voice* (1984) Brathwaite refers to creole or nation language as a 'submerged language'. It is 'submerged' because historically the African languages imported by slaves were proscribed by the European slave owner due to fear of slave insurrection. They were therefore pushed underground, although they continued to be spoken and to influence the development of Caribbean creoles. For Brathwaite and for other Caribbean writers, this history has given creole a uniquely subversive potential. Indeed, Nichols herself has spoken of creole being viewed as

15

inferior by the colonial powers when I was growing up, and [it] still has a social stigma attached to it in the Caribbean.

I think this is one of the main reasons why so many Caribbean poets, including myself, are now reclaiming our language heritage and exploring it. It's an act of spiritual survival on our part, the need (whether conscious or unconscious) to preserve something, that's important to us. It's a language that our foremothers and forefathers struggled to create and we're saying that it's a valid, vibrant language. We're no longer going to treat it with contempt or allow it to be misplaced.   (LN 97–8)

However, she stresses that this is not the only reason for her use of creole:

I find using it genuinely exciting. Some creole expressions are so vivid and concise, and have no equivalent in English ... I want something different; something that sounds and looks different to the eye on the page and to the ear. Difference, diversity and unpredictability make me tick.   (LN 98)

She has spoken in interview of being

excited by language ... I care about language ... It's the battle with language that I love. When it comes to writing poetry, it is the challenge of trying to create or chisel out a new language that I like. I like working in both standard English and creole. I tend to want to fuse the two tongues because I come from a background where the two worlds, creole and standard English, were constantly interacting ...   (LN 97)

Nichols says that her choice of language for a poem is not a conscious decision. Instead, 'The language, like the form and rhythm, dictates itself' (HT 297). Nichols's claim that 'when I'm writing creole it's a kind of creole that I naturally speak' signals the proximity of creole to a wider oral matrix, 'songs ... proverbs, rhythms and so on' (WH). Creole is thus in part a language of intimacy, familiarity and sincerity. However, all literary use of creole is necessarily the use of an adapted form. To cite just one example, despite the existence of well-respected dictionaries of Caribbean English since the 1960s, there is still no standard orthography for transcribing an essentially oral medium into a written one. This is not necessarily a disadvantage to the writer wanting to use nation language in his or her work. Indeed, Guyanese writer and critic, David Dabydeen has argued that:

> In the brokenness of language resides ... the capacity to be experimental with a language; it is almost like Shakespearean English. You can make up words, play with words and you can rhyme in much more adventurous ways than you can in standard English ... you can reconstruct in your own way, you can play with the language with a greater degree of freedom.[23]

Moreover, to use nation language is to access a possible range of timbres, rhythms and sounds that are simply not available to the poet in standard English. As Brathwaite suggests, referring to nation language: 'English it may be in terms of some of its lexical features. But in its contours, its rhythm and timbre, its sound explosions, it is not English'.[24] He continues:

> [Nation language] may be in English: but often it is in an English which is like a howl, or a shout or a machine-gun or the wind or a wave [as in Nichols's 'Sea Timeless Song, *FBW* 48]. It is also like the blues. And sometimes it is English and African at the same time.[25]

Ultimately Nichols's concern in her poetry is to 'create [her] own voice' but she admits, 'it isn't easy trying to capture something that is true to you. But it's what makes your poetry very ... distinctive' (*EF*) Nichols's use of standard English tends to predominate in those poems which explore the more painful aspects of diasporic life, such as 'Island Man' (*FBW* 29) or 'Two Old Black Men on a Leicester Square Park Bench' (*FBW* 35), although there are exceptions. Conversely the use of creole tends to occur within a strong celebratory context in which creole is validated not only as the language of intimacy and of tenderness but also of confident identity, vitality, solidarity and strength, as in a number of *The Fat Black Woman's Poems*. It is also used to great comic and satirical effect, although to see creole as functioning only in these contexts is to underestimate its tremendous potential as a creative medium.

READING GRACE NICHOLS (MORE SERIOUSLY)

Back in 1967 Jamaican poet and academic Mervyn Morris was pleading for the undervalued and misunderstood 'nation language' work of fellow Jamaican poet Louise Bennett to be taken more seriously.[26] Without needing to make quite the

17

same claims for Nichols, I do want to encourage more serious reading of her work. One recent critical summary of her work is a case in point. The entry on Nichols in *The Reader's Companion to Twentieth Century Writers*, edited by Peter Parker, describes *The Fat Black Woman's Poems* as a 'less planned and complete work' than *i is a long memoried woman*, even as it acknowledges that it 'adds the theme of the emigrant first arriving in England to a contemplation of childhood as seen through backward glances to the homeland'.[27]

In my own experience of teaching Nichols's poetry, I have also found students new to her work prone to making the charge that certain of Nichols's poems, especially in *The Fat Black Woman's Poems*, are simplistic, ineffectual or 'lightweight', and at worst 'not really [serious] poetry at all' – a charge which was also made against Bennett much earlier in the century; yet with a more informed understanding of the specific historical, cultural, literary and linguistic contexts in which Nichols's work can be read, the same students often glimpse a 'world of something'[28] which they had overlooked in their initial readings. This may be as simple as the cultural significance of the use of 'nation language' in Caribbean and black British poetry, or as complex as the historical freight of slavery and images of institutionalised racism which are so deftly incorporated into certain of Nichols's poems (e.g. the North American Aunt Jemima stereotype in 'The Fat Black Woman Remembers' (*FBW* 9), the use of the term 'Steatopygous', meaning 'an excess of fat on the buttocks' (*OED*) and originally used in relation to the infamous 'Hottentot Venus'[29] in 'Thoughts drifting through a fat black woman's head while having a full bubble bath' (*FBW* 15) or the similar significant reference to 'Bantu buttocks' in 'Configuration' (*LTLW* 31).

Interestingly, the charge of lack of seriousness or social commitment is one which Nichols herself recognizes and it led her to make the following response in 1988:

> I think I have a sense of humour ... It comes out in A Fat Black Woman, for example, and some people or critics can't seem to come to terms with it. People have said to me *i is a long memoried woman* is such a moving and deep book, and *The Fat Black Woman*, a few people have said, or told other poets, doesn't carry forward

18

the struggle . . . they see it as a frivolous book. It isn't – it's just that things are put in a funny way because the laughter and the humour is healing and is very much part of Caribbean people. I hate the one-dimensional stereotype of the black woman as just being a sufferer or a person who's a victim or who's had a very oppressive history and she's carrying all these scars on her back, because I know that not to be true. On one realistic level we have had, as black women, an oppressive history, and we . . . have had to bear more than our fair share of burdens, but I know so many black women who are such rich humorous human beings inside that I can't easily identify with that stereotype or image. In my writings I'm conscious of that – to give other pictures and other images of black women as distinct from being this victim figure or a person who's been extremely oppressed.   (MB 19)

As she suggests, humour can have a serious function and, conversely, political and aesthetic seriousness need not be completely 'po-faced' or humourless.[30]

Nichols makes similar points in her poem 'Of Course When They Ask for Poems About the "Realities" of Black Women' (*LTLW* 52–4). In 'Of Course . . .' her project is to deconstruct some stereotypical expectations of black women poetry and to draw attention to the problems of totalizing categories such as 'black women'. The poem opens:

> What they really want
> At times
> Is a specimen
> Whose heart is in the dust
>
> A mother-of-sufferer
> Trampled, oppressed
> They want a little black blood
> Undressed
> And validation
> For the abused stereotype
> Already in their heads

Moreover, as the persona points out:

> . . . there ain't no
> Easy-belly category
> For a black woman
> Or a white woman
> Or a green woman

19

Instead Nichols stresses the diversity within the homogenizing category of 'black women':

> And there are black women
> And black women
> Like a contrasting sky
> Of rainbow spectrum
>
> And there are black woman
> Strong and eloquent
> And focused
>
> And there are black women
> Who somehow always manage to end up
> Frail victim

The poem ends with the affirming vision of

> we black women
> full-of-we-selves walking
>
> Crushing out
> with each dancing step
> the twisted self-negating
> history
> we've inherited
> Crushing out
> With each dancing step.

There could be no better starting point for this study of Nichols and her writing.

2

Feminist Readings of Grace Nichols

> I am my own foundation. And it is by going beyond the historical, instrumental hypothesis that I will initiate the cycle of my freedom ... It is through the effort to recapture the self and to scrutinize the self ... that men will be able to create the ideal conditions of existence for a human world.
>
> – Frantz Fanon, *Black Skin:White Masks*[1]

> In order to perpetuate itself, every oppression must corrupt or distort those various sources of power within the culture of the oppressed that can provide energy for change. For women, this has meant a suppression of the erotic as a considered source of power and information within our lives ... the erotic is a resource within each of us.
>
> – Audre Lorde 'Uses of the Erotic: The Erotic as Power' (AL 53–4)

> Write your self. Your body must be heard
>
> – Hélène Cixous, 'The Laugh of the Medusa' (HC 320)

What links these three superficially quite dissimilar epigraphs is the idea of a concrete, bodily grounded, rather than abstractly defined self, as the 'foundation' and catalyst for change – whether in a colonial or a feminist context. French feminist Hélène Cixous's exhortation to women to 'Write your self. Your body must be heard', and her stress on the 'connection between the woman's body, whose sexual pleasure has been repressed and denied expression [for centuries under

21

patriarchal rule], and women's writing',[2] is a potent one. It is also one which is manifestly taken up in Nichols's poetry, and thus Cixous's influential essay is considered in relation to Nichols's writing in this chapter.

However, one might equally turn to a very different tradition of feminist writing and theorizing, an African-American one, for incisive insights on this centrally important characteristic of Nichols's poetry. Accordingly, the final part of this chapter looks at a selection of Nichols's poems in relation to Audre Lorde's 'Uses of the Erotic: The Erotic as Power'.[3] In this essay, Lorde reclaims the erotic from its popularly misconstrued, patriarchally determined meanings and argues for the erotic as an 'assertion of the lifeforce of women; of that creative energy empowered, the knowledge and use of which we are now reclaiming in our language, our history, our dancing, our loving, our work, our lives' (AL 53–4).

As early as the 1950s the Martiniquan-born psychiatrist and theorist Frantz Fanon, whose writing had emerged from his direct involvement in the revolutionary struggle against French colonial rule, in 1950s Algeria, argued for agency for the colonial subject, in terms which are not dissimilar to those used by Cixous and Lorde. Such intersections and imbrications between the female and the colonial (or postcolonial) subject lie at the heart of much of Nichols's poetry and are the focus of my analysis of the poem 'My Black Triangle' in this chapter. However, perhaps more importantly, these three voices (and especially that of Lorde) offer a salutary reminder that although poststructuralism has undermined the idea of a centred or unitary subject (as opposed to one produced as an effect of language, ideology, discourses) for some black (and some white) feminist critics, as for some postcolonial critics, thinking about the self in this way is still a crucial undertaking.

READING GRACE NICHOLS

Perhaps unsurprisingly, the little critical writing on Grace Nichols which does exist tends to draw upon insights from feminist and postcolonial theory. However, at the time of writing this book, no book-length postcolonial reading of

Nichols's work has yet been published and she features in surprisingly few collections of recent criticism of Caribbean women's writing. One has to turn to interviews and shorter critical pieces for discussion and analysis of Nichols's poetry within a dominantly postcolonial (including indigenous) theoretical framework.[4]

Feminist critiques of Nichols's work have been slightly more numerous. They include Jan Montefiore's analysis of *i is a long memoried woman* in *Feminism and Poetry* (1987), Gudrun Webhofer's study, *'Identity' in the Poetry of Grace Nichols and Lorna Goodison* (1996), and Gabriele Griffin's essay on *i is a long memoried woman* in *Black Women's Writing* (1993), all of which draw on the theories of French feminists such as Julia Kristeva, Anne Leclerc and Hélène Cixous.[5] Overall though, critical attention to Nichols is still not as widespread as one would expect, and Vicki Bertram has suggested that there may be theoretical reasons for this 'relative critical silence about Nichols' (PP 137). Bertram argues that 'the blindness' of certain theoretical perspectives and theory's 'lack of fit' to Nichols's poetry has led to the ignoring of her work in some cases.

This chapter deals with two very different feminist readings of Nichols's poetry. It considers how *i is a long memoried woman* can be productively read alongside 'The Laugh of the Medusa', Hélène Cixous's feminist manifesto for *écriture féminine* or feminine writing, and suggests new feminist readings of Nichols's work, reading key poems from *The Fat Black Woman's Poems* and from *Lazy Thoughts of a Lazy Woman* alongside Audre Lorde's essay 'The Uses of the Erotic'. It also looks closely at the kinds of reading strategies which can illuminate the complex intersection of race and gender issues in many of Nichols's poems, taking as its case study the poem 'My Black Triangle'.

Such readings are also intended to raise awareness of some important questions regarding the use of feminist theory in readings of black women's writing: the relation between texts and theory, the relative specificity or universalizing tendencies of certain theoretical approaches, and some different ways of conceptualizing the role and nature of theory itself. For example, what are the problems (as well as potentialities) of using European-derived feminist models to read women's writing from other cultures, and why have concepts from an African-American tradition of black feminist criticism been so under-utilized in critical readings of Nichols's work?

NICHOLS, FEMINISM AND CARIBBEAN WOMEN'S WRITING

Interestingly, one of the few explicit comments on feminism and writing that Nichols has made in interview falls comfortably within an Anglo-American tradition of feminist criticism which is materialist, politically grounded, interested in issues of 'real' power relations rather than more abstractly theoretical issues:

> I do see myself as a feminist writer; but seeing yourself as a feminist writer doesn't mean you're going to write books or stories just about women. Men are going to be there, very much so. But feminist [in] ... that there should be a rebalancing of power between men and women. Women, both black and white, have had an oppressive history where they've had to fight for so many rights ... Black women in particular have been neglected in literature. It's only within the last twenty years, since the women's movement, that in Europe you've had the upsurge of white women writers. You have presses like Virago, the Women's Press. In the Caribbean, where you don't have these kind of facilities, black women have had less opportunity to be published, for their voices to be heard. So from that point of view ... I'm also writing or speaking for black women also. (*CMB* 18)

On the one hand, Nichols's comments owe something to the gynocriticism of American feminist critics such as Elaine Showalter and their concern to explore the ways in which women have been both marginalized and represented in limiting ways within an androcentric literary tradition, and to uncover and encourage more awareness of more women's writing. On the other hand, her comments belong to a British – and significantly black British – feminist tradition of exposing and addressing the continuing constraints on women writers, from the politics of publishing to inequalities grounded in wider power relations in society. This more radical tradition is that to which Barbara Burford, Lauretta Ngcobo, Beverley Bryan, Stella Dadzie and Suzanne Scafe belong.

24

In a more recent interview, Nichols rejects being termed a feminist writer whilst openly acknowledging the centrality of a 'feminist philosophy' to her work, and the tremendous importance of the feminist movement internationally:

> I just wouldn't call myself a feminist writer. Nor would I simply say that I am a black writer ... Or that I am a woman writer, a Guyanese writer, or a postcolonial writer. They are all labels and at times they have a relevant context, depending on the situation you're in ... even though ... I don't call myself a feminist writer in that sense. Feminism and the idea of the feminist is very much part of my philosophy and what I have always believed in ... The feminist movement was important, you can't get away from that, in terms of the impact it has had around the world. In the past you might have had a big conference and you would find that all the writers were men. Now they are forced to take note, which is as it should be. We are now living in a complex culture, so you can't have the male Eurocentric voice defining what is literature all the time ... what belongs to the great canon of literature ... you have a much wider and varied kind of debate and communication going on. (KD 146–7)

One common misconception about Caribbean literature that was still prevalent until relatively recently was the belief that Caribbean women's writing 'emerged' for the first time only in the 1970s. However, as is so often the case historically with women's writing, this was an issue of in/visibility rather than an absence of writers and writing. As the editors of *The Routledge Reader in Caribbean Literature* pointed out in 1996: 'the fact that women writers have not been heard in an international context does not mean that they have been voiceless' (D&LW 17).

Amongst the many factors which have effectively militated against greater visibility for Caribbean women's writing are the perceptions of the women themselves (that writing wasn't an 'acceptable' occupation for a woman, that their writing was not really significant, or at least not worthy of publication or preservation for future generations). Caribbean women writers have, historically, been marginalized in relation to a powerfully androcentric canon, and the critical paradigms which emerged have traditionally been geared towards the work of male writers. Moreover, there is also a history of critical neglect of all but a small number of well-known and/or contemporary women writers. Nichols acknowledges that women in the Caribbean have always written, always been creative, but suggests that their writing and their creativity has not always been fully recognized or visible.[6] She credits the feminist movement as an important contributory factor in facilitating a more visible and confident Caribbean women's writing:

> writing don't happen in a vacuum ... [but] to create you need that whole climate around you in which you can feel empowered and ... a sense of freedom which women haven't had in the Caribbean ... Take my mother's generation, for example – she was a talented woman in her own right; she played the piano and so on, but she had seven children and was completely economically dependent on her husband. A lot of women were like that. They weren't really going into the professions, and certainly, writing would not have been seen as a career in which to make a living. But some of these women might quietly have poems tucked away, women of an older generation, and never would do anything about it. But to name yourself as a writer and come out and really perform your poetry on stage, and bring out records, and try to get published, would have been something that would have been alien to their generation, because ... writing especially for a woman (for a man it's always been easier to name yourself as an artist) it's seen as a bit presumptuous ... Being able to make a living from it would not have been an easy thing to do for a lot of women. So you needed a feminist movement, you needed lots of things to happen for this emergence of women because women have been writing in the past, but might have kept it quiet and certainly would not have been making a living from it as lots of women writers I know in England are doing today ... I think those factors contributed towards a whole feeling of freedom, psychically and creatively and in every way. But why it only happened in the last fifteen, twenty years is interesting. So that's why I'm saying that it's also related to the broader developments in the broader society. And the feminist movement was a big contribution ... (KD 143)

Part of Nichols's reluctance to label herself a feminist writer may possibly stem from what Kwame Dawes has termed the

> rather ambivalent position towards western feminism ... [taken by] many of our women poets ... ambivalent because while there is an open unwillingness to be labelled a feminist writer, these writers, clearly because of their radical position on issues of gender, are challenging the status quo. (KD 146)

26

Such 'open unwillingness to be labelled a feminist writer' is clearly partially a matter of individual choice. However, it also reflects a history of popular attitudes in the Caribbean whereby feminism and feminist theory have sometimes been viewed as 'foreign imports', something which infiltrates the region from outside. Françoise Lionnet cites Lloyd Brown's sceptical comments on radical feminism and his residual suspicion of feminist approaches in the Caribbean, in his introduction to a 1984 collection of conference papers, as symptomatic of this tendency to see feminism as 'still largely foreign to the culture of the region'.[7] Brown argues that:

> The need to address Caribbean literature and society through feminist and pro-feminist perspectives has been longstanding and embarrassingly neglected, but attributing some sort of mass 'radicalism' to a pervasively conservative, often reactionary, society is quite another thing. There is the possibility that the exercise can be little more than the smuggling in of so much foreign (North American) baggage rather than a demonstrated reality of West Indian life.[8]

The defensive language of Lloyd's introduction, with its figures of covert (and illegal) importation of 'foreign [theoretical] baggage' has thankfully been replaced by a less volatile and more sophisticated approach to this issue. Patricia Mohammed, for example, in a recent essay entitled 'Towards Indigenous Feminist Theorising in the Caribbean' attempts to 'develop an indigenous reading of feminism as both activism and discourse in the Caribbean ... informed by my own preoccupation with the limits of contemporary postmodern feminist theorizing in terms of its accessibility, as well as application to understanding the specificity of a region'.[9] As such, she is one of a growing number of Caribbean feminist critics and historians, including Sylvia Wynter, Evelyn O'Callaghan, Patricia Mohammed, Rhoda Reddock, Bridget Brereton and Olive Senior, who are disrupting the simple polarities of Brown's 'foreign-native' opposition and proving that the Caribbean can have its own traditions of feminist and gender analyses that draw upon but are not necessarily complicit with, uncritical of or unresistant to, dominant Anglo-American approaches.

27

Anglo-American feminist criticism, as Nichols suggests, was clearly instrumental in initially opening up a liberal space in the West in which the nature, politics and poetics of women's writing could be debated and theorized, and wider issues of gender and sexuality considered. However, it has been fiercely critiqued in relation to its marginalization or exclusion of certain groups of women. More than one critic has commented on the effective exclusion of all but a handful of black writers from an emergent feminist literary canon, overwhelmingly white and Anglo-American in character, and the specific 'blindspots' of Anglo-American feminist theory with regard to black and lesbian subjectivities, modes of association and creativity have been similarly noted,[10] as have the wider issues arising from what Simmonds calls the 'whiteness of theory'.[11]

This chapter gives space to both white and black feminist theorists without intending to juxtapose them in any simplistically polarized or essentialized way (i.e. this is the 'white' reading practice versus the 'black' reading practice). Such oppositionalities are not only unsustainable but also unhelpful and damaging. However, it is worth bearing in mind the disproportionate visibility – and thus hegemonic position – of many Western feminist theorists in relation to indigenous theorists and to those who theorize in different ways. In an often cited passage, Caribbean-born, African-American feminist theorist Barbara Christian reminds us that Western models are not the only available models for theorizing:

> People of color have always theorized – but in forms quite different from the Western form of abstract logic. And I am inclined to say that our theorising . . . is often in narrative forms, in the stories we create, in riddles and proverbs, in the play with language, since dynamic rather than fixed ideas seem more to our liking . . .[12]

WRITING THE BODY: THE SEXUAL AND THE TEXTUAL

A number of feminist critics have been drawn to the striking yoking of the sexual and the textual, the erotic and the poetic in Nichols's work. They note the heightened awareness of the female body, and particularly female sexuality, in Nichols's work, and the way in which it is linked to a wider sense of creative empowerment and confident selfhood in her poetry.[13] For example, Webhofer argues that: 'for Nichols ... female identity is bound with physical experience: Grace Nichols represents the body both as a reality and as a signifier of sexual identity; besides she makes a libidinal force responsible for poetic creativity' (GWI 76).

Nichols's comment that, for her, 'poetry, thankfully is a radical synthesising force. The erotic isn't separated from the political or spiritual' (LN 103) proves especially useful to critics such as Webhofer, who draw upon French feminist theory in their reading of the poetry. This is because it echoes the intimate relationship between women's bodies and their writing, or more precisely, between women's sexuality, libidinal drives and experiences of sexual pleasure, and their use of language, which is postulated by feminist theorists such as Hélène Cixous and Julia Kristeva.

For Webhofer, Nichols's poetry exemplifies *l'écriture féminine*:[14] Webhofer stresses Cixous's emphasis on the role of the woman's body when she speaks in public: 'she physically materialises what she's thinking: she signifies it with her body ... because she doesn't deny her drives, the ... part they have in speaking' (HC 321) and the notion of the body as text: 'Text: my body – shot through with streams of song ... that part of you that leaves a space between yourself and urges you to inscribe in language your woman's' style' (HC 322). She also finds Cixous's argument that female speech 'lacks that scission, that division made ... between the logic of oral speech and the logic of the text' (HC 322) useful in considering the oral aspects of Nichols's writing as a woman poet from the Caribbean, where there are long traditions of oracy and different forms of orally based expression.

For both Webhofer and Griffin, Nichols 'demonstrates the notion of writing the body by creating difference on the page: by the unconventional layout and style and by the oral quality of her poems' (GWI 76). Griffin observes that the poems in *i is a long memoried woman*

> are aligned to an oral tradition which takes its rhythms and its inflections from the body. Breaks are recreated not by punctuation but by the need to draw breath, by how the body moves as it

recited ... The body of the texts is only very sparingly marked by the signs that come from a written tradition of language usage such as commas, question marks, dots. In fact, nothing comes to an end with a full stop: there is no stopping the revolution. It is not over. (GG 26).

Griffin demonstrates this with readings of 'Drum-Spell', 'Hi de Buckras Hi!' and 'Your Blessing' from *i is*. She suggests that the 'rhythmic incantations and repetitions' in these poems 'signal the *semiotic* disposition,''the body in process'' as Kristeva describes it, the defiance of the authority of imposed, alien structures' (GG 33). In this way the form of the poems mirrors their subject matter. Such poems are also examples of 'writing the body' since their 'appeal is not purely cerebral ... [they] need ... to be performed ... require ... the presence of the voice and the body.' (GG 33)

However, it is also worth considering some of the problems of this kind of reading of Nichols's work. Even if we accept that something which we might term *l'écriture féminine* is possible, and many critics do not,[15] there are certain problems inherent in mobilizing such concepts in a critical reading of actual women's texts. Griffin's discussion of Nichols's poem cycle as 'in many respects the perfect example of an *écriture féminine*'[16] provides some useful insights but also produces some startling generalizations and essentialisms; this is arguably one of the dangers inherent in attempting to apply certain highly figurative concepts from French feminist theory to specific women's texts. Despite using such concepts herself, Webhofer makes a similar point when she argues that

Nichols sometimes runs the risk of being misunderstood: especially the poems of ... [*LTLW*] may give the impression that Nichols is reducing woman's nature and creative ability to her physicality. This could be the case if we understand the metaphors concerning the body literally ... a danger enhanced, in my view, by the rather vaguely defined metaphors, which French Feminist Theory provides as tools for describing women's writing.[17]

A further problem is the tendency for feminist theorists to gravitate towards black women's texts as the grounded, historicized examples for their theory and to reinscribe the centuries-old association of the black woman with the body, with 'experience, sensuality, emotion, matter, practice as opposed to theory, and survival'.[18] In Margaret Homans's words, 'black women have been required to do the cultural work of embodying the body for white culture'.[19] She cites African-American critic Valerie Smith's identification of 'a disturbing trend': the use of black women writers by white feminists (as well as black men) to represent the ground of experience, or as Smith puts it, 'to rematerialize the subject of their theoretical positions'.[20] Smith observes:

> That the black woman appears in all of these texts as a historicizing presence testifies to the power of the insistent voices of black feminist literary and cultural critics. Yet it is striking that at precisely the moment when Anglo-American feminists and male Afro-Americans begin to reconsider the material ground of their enterprise, they demonstrate their return to earth, as it were, by invoking the specific experiences of black women and the writings of black women. This association of black women with reembodiment resembles rather closely the association, in classic Western philosophy and in nineteenth-century cultural constructions of womanhood, of women of color with the body and therefore with animal passions and slave labor.[21]

Both Webhofer's and Griffin's readings of Nichols's poetry suffer, at times, from being insufficiently located in a specific cultural context and from a tendency to fall back on generalizations about black women's writing which act to subsume the differences between black women writers from African, the Caribbean and different diasporic locations. For example, Webhofer argues that:

> For either poet identity is closely bound up with a sense of community: both believe that a Caribbean female subject can be forged only if women act as a collective. The black women in their poems draw strength from female bonding and through reference to myth and similar bodies of knowledge. Unlike the heroes in the works of writers from a liberal humanist tradition who assert identity through individuation, the characters in these poems find their self in community. (GWI 76)

Griffin too asserts that 'Eventually, in the course of time and history, [the long memoried woman] acquires a new identity bound up closely with the body and her power of speech' (GG

26), citing the epilogue to the poem cycle. Such statements show little cognisance of how specifically *i is* reflects the history of the complex language situation in the Caribbean; the 'new' tongue here is the creole tongue, the old the African. What for Griffin is a straightforward replacement of the old with the new, in a Caribbean literary context yields much more complex tensions and ambivalences; echoing the opening to Derek Walcott's poem dedicated to Kamau Brathwaite, 'Names'.[22] Nichols's epilogue registers not only Walcott's poetic sense of elation in the new world, the poet's 'awe of the numinous [and] elemental privilege of naming the New World' but also the 'bitter memory of migration', 'the mixture of the acid and the sweet'[23] or, in Brathwaite's words, the creolized tongue (and culture) of the Caribbean as 'some-/thing torn/ and new'.[24]

Griffin's reading shows little acknowledgement of the problematics of applying Western theory to black women's texts from different cultural traditions. Nor does her reading recognize that the Caribbean has its own traditions and figures of female resistance (such as Nanny of the Maroons[25] who features in Nichols's poem cycle, *i is*) as well as culturally specific terms and concepts (such as the Jamaican notion of the 'Tallawah woman', or the use of the term mac'mere (or macumere) to signify good female friends) which cannot be easily translated or accommodated by this Western feminist theoretical apparatus.[26] These are just some of the problems raised by feminist readings of this kind.

Paraskevi Papaleonida engages with similar issues, in a recent essay on the work of Jackie Kay and Nichols.[27] Her essay takes as its starting point Vicki Bertram's valuable recognition that in the face of

> a multitude of Gods and Goddesses from cultures throughout the world . . . a flood of unfamiliar rhythms, images and visions in the poetry being written in many languages that take their roots from the same form of 'English . . . [t]he old tools of critical exegesis are hopefully inadequate'.[28]

She argues that 'since not all readings (and especially not one reading) are good for all texts, particular texts need particular readings and no one reading [should] be used for "postcolonial literature" as a whole' (PP 136). Interestingly, Web-hofer does not choose to focus on what seems to me a highly illuminating insight from Cixous's 'Laugh of the Medusa'. Cixous writes that woman's 'writing her self ... is the invention of a new insurgent writing which, when the moment of her liberation has come, will allow her to carry out the indispensable ruptures and transformations in her history' (HC 320); this 'act ... will also be marked by woman's *seizing* the occasion to speak, hence her shattering entry into history, which has always been based on her *suppression*' (HC 321). Cixous could be writing here of the long memoried woman or the protagonist of 'sunris' and their epic journeyings; her comments can also be seen as insightful in a gendered context (writing as a woman) and in a Caribbean historical and cultural context too.

NICHOLS AND THE USES OF THE EROTIC

Nichols's poetry is full of echoes, allusions, even dedications to African-American women writers, particularly Ntozake Shange and Audre Lorde, although very few critics seem to have commented on this. The final part of this chapter looks at a selection of Nichols's poems in relation to one such writer's important and highly illuminating essay: Audre Lorde's 'Uses of the Erotic: The Erotic as Power'.

Lorde's subject in this essay is 'the many kinds of power, used and unused, acknowledged or otherwise' (AL 53). She argues:

> The erotic is a resource within each of us and lies in a deeply female and spiritual plane, firmly rooted in the power of our unexpressed or unrecognized feeling. In order to perpetuate itself, every oppression must corrupt or distort those various sources of power within the culture of the oppressed that can provide energy for change. For women, this has meant a suppression of the erotic as a considered source of power and information within our lives
> . . .
> We have been taught to suspect this resource, vilified, abused and devalued within western society ... On the one hand, the superficially erotic has been encouraged as a sign of female

inferiority; on the other hand, women have been made to suffer and to feel contemptible and suspect by virtue of its existence. (AL 53–4).

Lorde's project in 'The Use of the Erotic' is to restore the 'erotic' to women as a positive 'replenishing and provocative force'. She notes how 'the erotic has often been misnamed by men and used against women' (AL 54), confused 'with its opposite, the pornographic', which she defines as emphasizing sensation rather than feeling. In this essay she attempts to open up the term 'erotic' by liberating it from narrow definitions linked to sex. Instead, she links the erotic to women's creativity, 'self-connection' (through one's body and those of others) and satisfaction in a range of wider contexts. In Lorde's words: 'When I speak of the erotic . . . I speak of it as an assertion of the lifeforce of women; of that creative energy empowered, the knowledge and use of which we are now reclaiming in our language, our history, our dancing, our loving, our work, our lives' (AL 55). For her, the erotic is 'not a question only of what we do; it is a question of how acutely and fully we can feel in the doing' (AL 54).

What makes the erotic so important to Lorde as a feminist is its transformative potential:

> Once we know the extent to which we are capable of feeling that sense of satisfaction and completion, we can then observe which of our various life endeavors brings us closest to that fullness . . . Our erotic knowledge . . . becomes a lens through which we scrutinize all aspects of our existence, forcing us to evaluate those aspects honestly in terms of their relative meaning within our lives. And this is a grave responsibility, projected from within each of us, not to settle for the convenient, the shoddy, the conventionally expected, nor the merely safe. (AL 54–5, 57)

Making use of the erotic in this way, is therefore an empowering force for women and doubly so given that it is an inner resource. 'Women so empowered are dangerous', Lorde suggests, or at least they are regarded as such by the patriarchal establishment. She argues that this is why women 'are taught to separate the erotic from most vital areas of our lives other than sex' and that this leads to 'disaffection from so much of what we do' (AL 55). Lorde concludes her essay with the assertion:

34

Recognizing the power of the erotic within our lives can give us the energy to pursue genuine change within our world . . . for not only do we touch our most profoundly creative source, but we do that which is female and self-affirming in the face of a racist, patriarchal, and anti-erotic society'. (AL 59)

Lorde's essay is more than pertinent to a reading of Nichols's *The Fat Black Woman's Poems*. Indeed, it can be argued that Nichols's generic 'Fat Black Woman' exemplifies the use of the erotic as power in her confrontation with a similarly 'racist, patriarchal, and anti-erotic society' in Britain. 'Beauty', the first poem of this collection, overturns white, Eurocentric ideals of beauty, as beauty is instead personified as:

> a fat black woman
> walking the fields
> pressing a breezed
> hibiscus
> to her cheek
> while the sun lights up
> her feet
>
> (FBW 7)[29]

The image is of a woman who is larger than life, not just literally, but in terms of her goddess-like stature and magnificence. Our reading of this first stanza, which might otherwise have seemed merely to peddle an idealized image of the woman as exotic 'other', is thus subtly altered. This construction and dismantling of familiar stereotypes of black women is one of Nichols's recurrent techniques in *The Fat Black Woman's Poems* and *Lazy Thoughts of a Lazy Woman*.[30]

In 'Looking at Miss World' (*FBW* 20) Nichols explores similar issues in a more concrete form. The fat black woman watches the eponymous international beauty contest, 'await[ing] in vain' for 'some Miss (plump at least/ if not fat and black [to] uphold her name' (*FBW* 20). Instead, Nichols describes the contestants in a typically witty fashion, through the punning use of the term 'bare' and the oxymoronic 'hopeful despair' as 'slim after slim aspirant appears/ baring her treasures in hopeful despair' (*FBW* 20). Whereas the fat black woman is aggravated by 'de pretty face salesgals/ exchanging slimming glances/ thinking she don't notice' in

'The Fat Black Woman Goes Shopping', in this poem, she is serene, dignified and empowered in the face of so much superficial beauty. She recognizes that, although 'the beauties yearn', they never get to really 'burn' (*FBW* 20). The use of the erotic as power, in Lorde's sense, has not been realized by the contestants; instead, as the phrase, 'hopeful despair' suggests, they are still under 'the spell of too much male white power',[31] in thrall to the prevailing ideals of physical beauty determined by a 'racist, patriarchal, and anti-erotic society' (AL 59). Significantly, the fat black woman is neither passive nor silent in the face of this spectacle. She gets up 'And pours some gin/ Toasting herself as a likely win' (*FBW* 20).

Nichols's comment that, for her, 'poetry, thankfully is a radical synthesising force. The erotic isn't separated from the political or spiritual' (LN 103) proves especially useful to a feminist reading which seeks to look at her work alongside Lorde's essay. Lorde similarly writes that 'the dichotomy between the spiritual and the political is . . . false . . . the bridge which connects is formed by the erotic – the sensual – those physical, emotional, and psychic expressions of what is deepest and strongest and richest within each of us, being shared' (AL 56).

One of the clearest expressions of this connection between the erotic and the political or spiritual in Nichols's poetry is 'My Black Triangle', which is discussed in fuller detail at the end of this chapter. In this poem 'Nichols represents the body both as a reality and as a signifier of sexual identity; besides she makes a libidinal force responsible for poetic creativity' (GuW 76). The black triangle can be read as a metonym for the fertile potential of the female body and for the transformative power of female sexual desire; as such it is intimately linked to a wider, even cosmic, sense of a creative force in the poem. The spontaneous fluidity of 'writing the body' is deliberately contrasted to the sterility of patriarchal discourse:

> my black triangle
> is so rich
> that it flows
> on to the dry crotch
> of the world . . .

> my black triangle
> has spread beyond his story
> beyond the dry fears of parch-ri-archy
>
> (*LTLW* 25)

Certainly the poem seems to demonstrate Lorde's belief that when we realize the power of the erotic 'we touch our most profoundly creative source ... female and self-affirming' (AL 59). This is particularly evident in the concluding lines: 'my black triangle/ carries the seal of approval/ of my deepest self' (AL 25).

Another poem which exemplifies the link between the erotic, the political and the spiritual is 'On Poems and Crotches', dedicated to the poet Ntozake Shange:

> Just tinkin bout/
> How hot it isht/
> Tween yo crotch/
> Isht enuf/
> To make you rush/
> To rite a poem/
>
> For poems are born
> In the bubbling soul of the crotch
> Poems hug Visionary-Third-Eye.
> Kiss Intellect.
> Before hurrying on down
> To burst their way through the crotch.
>
> Women who love their crotches
> Will rise
> Higher and higher ...
>
> Will create out of the vast silence.
>
> (*LTLW* 16)

Here, the link between women's literature and women's libido is even more explicit, as 'poems are born/ In the bubbling soul of the crotch'. The latter is an interesting image, which destabilizes the patriarchal binary opposition that conventionally links women to the body and to physicality, and men to the intellect or mind and to spirituality. In 'On Poems and Crotches' the crotch is ironically described as a 'bubbling soul'; writing the body, realizing the creative power of the erotic, are offered as alternative, woman-centred means of making poems. And, as the poem intimates, the work of such poets will carry a tremendous political force as they emerge from a perceived 'vast silence' of women's voices.

UNPACKING 'MY BLACK TRIANGLE'

I want now to look at one of Nichols's best-known poems, 'My Black Triangle' from *Lazy Thoughts of a Lazy Woman* (1989), as a short case study in the kind of feminist and postcolonial reading practices which can be productively used to demonstrate the complex intersection of racial and gender concerns in Nichols's poetry. I also consider a number of other poems from this collection and from *The Fat Black Woman's Poems* in which an understanding of the complex legacies of representation of the female and racial body is crucial.

In 'My Black Triangle' (*LTLW* 25) Nichols overlays different connotations of the black triangle. Historically, 'the black triangle' was a term used to refer to the three-way 'traffic' of raw materials, manufactured goods and slaves of the Atlantic slave trade. Europeans traded manufactured cotton goods, small hardware and metalwork products and firearms from their own countries, for African slaves along the west coast of Africa; this human freight of African slaves was then transported from Africa to the Caribbean in order to provide labour forces for the great plantations of the New World (the Americas and the Caribbean); and the third and final leg of the black triangle involved the export of produce such as sugar, tobacco, cotton and coffee, from the New World plantations back to Europe to be processed and ultimately consumed there. However, the 'black triangle', in Nichols's poem, is also a reference to the female pudenda.

Such a yoking of historical experience and gendered image reminds us that the slave experience, too, was importantly also a gendered experience, one which encompassed quite specific fears, losses and oppressions for the female slave. 'The black woman was situated at the (re)productive core of the slave system with a unique legal status':[32] any children she might bear took on slave status at birth, regardless of the status of the father and thus provided an additional economic incentive to the widespread sexual as well as racial abuse of black slave women at the hands of the white overseer and plantation owner; moreover, the status of her children as property meant that they could be forcibly removed to plantations or sold to other owners. Slavery undoubtedly 'damaged' the gender identities of both men and women, but as Patricia Morton has argued, the gulfs between black and white women, and the crucial differences in the experiences of enslaved men and women, meant that 'black women confronted the master's power in "ultimate loneliness"'.[33]

The black triangle of Nichols's poem is, as Webhofer observes, 'the seat of erotic pleasure but ... also has connotations of the dark continent, of an unknown, unexplored territory' (GWI 14). It thus yokes together two further traces of meaning in the one black female body: the late-Victorian use of the metaphor 'dark continent' to describe Africa (as in Joseph Conrad's *Heart of Darkness*) and Sigmund Freud's use of the metaphor to describe female sexuality. Interestingly, Cixous appropriates precisely this damaging metaphor of female sexuality and abrogates its power in 'The Laugh of the Medusa'. For Cixous and other French feminists such as Julia Kristeva whose writings are influenced by the psychoanalytical theories of Jacques Lacan, the child's entry into language is crucial to the process of socialization into gender roles. Cixous argues: 'As soon as [little girls] begin to speak, at the same time as they're taught their name, they can be taught that their territory is black: because you are Africa, you are black. Your continent is dark. Dark is dangerous. You can't see anything in the dark, you're afraid . . .' (HC 318).

Pursuing the connections between the suppression of women's sexuality and sexual pleasure, and their writing, in metaphorical terms, she counters: 'the Dark Continent is neither dark nor unexplorable. It is still unexplored only because we've been made to believe that it was too dark to be explorable. And they [i.e. men] want to make us believe that what interests us is the white continent, with its monuments to Lack' (HC 325).

Cixous's appropriation and abrogation of Freud's terms 'dark continent' is fascinating, but what she fails to address in her essay are its implications for black women writers. It is difficult to ascertain how Cixous's metaphors might translate in relation to black female subjects for whom the metaphorical ascription 'the Dark Continent' is altogether more complex and multilayered than for the white woman, and who seem excluded here. The collusion of whiteness and phallocentrism/ patriarchy in Cixous's phrase 'the white continent, with its monuments to Lack' is also problematic when considered within this new context.

That aside, it is possible to see Nichols's black female persona exercising a similar kind of appropriation and abrogation of the metaphor of the black triangle. She seizes control over the process of signification, by personalizing the metaphor ('*my* black triangle') and by stressing its close connection to the female body, allowing it to signify wider possibilities and more positive attributes: the ability to 'experience the world [and one's own history] through [the] body' (GWI 14), to celebrate the creative potential for growth ('Spreading and growing/ trusting and flowing', *LTLW* 25) and the empowering nature of confident female sexuality, self-affirming and approving 'of my deepest self' (*LTLW* 25).

An initial reading of 'Thoughts drifting through the fat black woman's head while having a full bubble bath' (*FBW* 15) might lead one to conclude that this is merely a domesticized and altogether more satirical treatment of the issues raised by other poems in the *Fat Black Woman's Poems* collection. However, in this and other poems, Nichols alludes to a longer history of representing the black female body which is crucial to an understanding of the poem. The poem opens with the remarkable lines: 'Steatopygous sky/ Steatopygous sea/ Steatopygous waves/ Steatopygous me' (*FBW* 15). *The Concise Oxford English Dictionary* defines 'Steatopygous' as having 'excessive development of fat on the buttocks, especially of Hottentot [or Khoi-Khoi people of southern Africa] woman'. It originated in anthropological discourse of the eighteenth century and was most famously used to refer to Sarah Bartmann (Saartje Baartman), a black indentured servant of the eighteenth century who became known as 'The Hottentot Venus'. Baartman aroused great curiosity due to her steatopygia and hypertrophic labia (artificially enlarged external genitalia) and was publicly displayed in Paris and London over a five-year period before her early death in 1815. After her death she was dissected more than once and her buttocks and labia (those parts which, it was argued, were evidence of black women's excessive sexual appetites) remained on display until the mid 1970s in the Musée de l'Homme in Paris.[34]

In choosing to use such a precise term, Nichols historicizes the fat black woman's situation. Her subversive longing:

> to place my foot
> on the head of anthropology
>
> to swig my breasts
> in the face of history
>
> to scrub my back
> with the dogma of theology
>
> (FBW 15)

stages an imagined confrontation between the hugely influential (largely white, male) discourses that have traditionally represented the black, female body, and an actual black woman, using the power of the erotic to re-centre herself as the agent, as the subject not object of this poem. 'Steatopygous' is, in a sense, rehabilitated by the fat black woman's appropriation; although it carries the 'pain of history' it is also used as a positive term of self-identification, as the fat black woman realizes in her own body a history of representing the black female form. This is what Michel Foucault would term an example of reverse-discourse.

Nichols alludes to the iconographic significance of the black female buttocks more fleetingly in 'Invitation' (FBW 13), another poem in which the power of the erotic is fully realized by a fat black woman, centred and confident in her own body:

> my breasts are huge exciting
> amnions of watermelon
>   your hands can't cup
> my thighs are twin seals
>   fat slick pups
> there's a purple cherry
> below the blues
>   of my black seabelly

41

> there's a mole that gets a ride
> each time I shift the heritage
> of my behind
>
> come up and see me sometime.
>
> (*FBW* 13)

Here, the use of the term '*heritage/* of my behind' is highly significant, yet it is often overlooked in readings of the poem.

The concluding line is also interesting in its appropriation of the most famous quip of Hollywood actress Mae West. Having the fat black women quote a fat white woman on the art of seduction makes for a fascinating political situation.[35] Both women are equally confident in their sexuality but are nonetheless positioned very differently in terms of their status, visibility, their access to power and, crucially, to the machinery of representation.

In the more complex poem 'Configurations' (*LTLW* 31), the backside as the most celebrated part of the black female anatomy resurfaces as the black woman's 'Bantu buttocks'. 'Configurations' stages an encounter between a white man and a black woman, in order to explore the sexual politics of the encounter between Europe and Africa (*LTLW* 31).[36]

One final poem which charts a different aspect of the complex legacies of representations of the black female body is 'The Fat Black Woman Remembers' (*FBW* 9). In this poem, it is more recent nineteenth- and twentieth-century stereotypes of the 'Fat Black Mama' or 'Jovial Jemima' that Nichols alludes to, most famously realized in the character of the cook in the film *Gone with the Wind*, and immortalized as the disembodied housekeeper in hundreds of *Tom and Jerry* cartoons, as well as featuring in the advertising for a number of American-produced food products of the twentieth century.[37]

> The fat black woman
> remembers her Mama
> and them days of playing
> the Jovial Jemima
>
> tossing pancakes
> to heaven
> in smokes of happy hearty

> murderous blue laughter
>
> Starching and cleaning . . .
> pressing little white heads
> against her big-aproned breasts . . .

(FBW 9)

The implication of 'playing' is that this is a subservient role that black women have been forced into playing since their earliest experiences in America as house-slaves and later on as domestic servants. They played the role in order to survive and earn their livelihoods within the strict racial hierarchy of these societies. However, as in other of Nichols's poems such as 'Skin Teeth' (*ILMW* 50) the fat black Mama's laughter is double-edged: 'happy hearty' but also 'murderous' (*FBW* 9). Whilst her Mama may desire to break out of the white stereotype of 'Jovial Jemima', the fat black woman states more assertively: 'But this fat black woman ain't no Jemima/ Sure thing Honey/ Yeah' (*FBW* 9).

FEMINIST READINGS . . . AND FEMINIST READINGS

There are clearly points of contact and overlap between the two feminist reading strategies for Nichols's writing discussed in this chapter. However, the politics of Lorde's positioning as a feminist theorist may be more 'usable' in this context than Cixous's. This is not simply a matter of race. To argue that we should only, or should necessarily, use insights from black feminist theory simply because we are considering the work of a black woman poet would be an essentialist move which may not only prove unsustainable in practice but be singularly unhelpful in a reading of a given work. A theoretically informed reading should open up possibilities for reading literature, not close them down. Moreover, to paraphrase Paraskevi Papaleonida's point quoted earlier in the chapter, not all theories fit all texts.

However, Lorde's does seem to be the more enabling position. Partly this is due to the distancing and homogenizing effects of Cixous's theories, like those of a number of other French feminists. Her writing, although intentionally playful

43

and poetic, tends to deal in abstractions, and to elide difference between women under the homogenizing effects of 'Woman'. In contrast, Lorde's writing springs out of an immediate and politicized context in which the voice must literally be heard. Indeed, 'Uses of the Erotic' started out as a conference paper and retains many of the markers of oral communication even in written form.

Perhaps, ultimately, to speak for oneself is better than being spoken for. Indeed, Lorde repeatedly stresses that silence is defeat and that only by speaking out can women empower themselves and liberate themselves from the oppressive structures of representation which surround and define them. Moreover, within a postcolonial context to be able to speak oneself (in both senses of the word: oneself and one's self) is crucial if your history has been an oppressive one of being elided or pushed to the margins, of being silenced or not being heard, of being in the recent words of Halle Berry, the first ever African-American woman to win an Oscar (in 2002): 'one of the nameless, faceless, women of color'.

Clearly, both feminist readings have their potentialities and their pitfalls. The solution may be to 'border-cross' theoretically too, to recognize that a hybridized approach which draws upon Cixous's collapsing of patriarchal binary oppositions in 'writing the body' and Lorde's more politicized reading strategies in relation to the 'erotic', may be the most enabling.[38]

44

3

Epic Journeying I: *i is a long memoried woman*

Soon we must make a journey . . .
Into the heart. Wherever the spiral memory
leads our dreaming feet.

> – 'Behind the Mask', LTLW, 55–6)

I am here
a woman . . . with all my lives
strung out like beads . . .
a woman charting my own futures/ a woman
holding my beads in my hand.

> – 'Holding My Beads', ILMW 86

We . . . have to come up with new myths . . . [we need to]
keep on creating and reshaping.

> – LN 101–2

This chapter foregrounds readings which locate Nichols's writing within a primarily Caribbean and/or diasporic black British context and which show how she is influenced by, and draws upon, alter/native resources that may not always be familiar to all readers. Indeed, that *i is a long memoried woman* needs to be read within a specifically Caribbean context is suggested by Nichols's own comments on the genesis of the poem:

i is a long memoried woman in fact owes its inspiration to a dream I had one night of a young African girl swimming from Africa to the Caribbean with a garland of flowers around her. When I woke up I interpreted the dream to mean that she was trying to cleanse the ocean of the pain and suffering that her ancestors had gone through in that crossing from Africa to the New World . . . (HT 298)

I have an actual little poem in the book which is the first thing I wrote and the whole cycle grew around it . . . (R3F)[1]

[The cycle] began at a dreamlike, psychic level. It didn't begin with any didactic intentions at all. But as the book progressed, obviously, I had to go back and do a bit of research into things, to refresh my own mind on the history. (KD 138)

The nature of this journey(ing) is, then, at once mythic and real, singular and multiple but, significantly, its historical basis and its geography are quite precise. Nichols's 'young African girl swimming from Africa to the Caribbean' retraces the path of many millions of Africans who were sold into slavery, often by other Africans ('traded by men/ the colour of my own skin', *ILMW* 18) and transported to America and the Caribbean. There, as in Nichols's poem, those who had survived the horrors of 'the Middle Passage', the sea crossing to the New World (see 'Eulogy'), were put to work on the plantations to produce sugar and other commodities for export back to Europe.

In her introduction to *Kicking Daffodils*, Vicki Bertram notes that Nichols is 'one of the first generation of Caribbean poets to have had some indigenous models to offset the influence of the colonial education syllabus'.[2] This chapter draws upon elements of feminist and postcolonial theory in its concern with rewriting and revisionist mythmaking. However, it also offers new readings of Nichols's poetry which are attentive to exactly the kind of 'indigenous models' Bertram speaks of and which are so often neglected in criticism of Nichols's work.

One of the recurrent motifs of postcolonial literature, as Diana Brydon and Helen Tiffin have pointed out, is that of the journey or quest.[3] Not only are postcolonial writers concerned to interrogate and to 'rewrite . . . the European narratives of quest, discovery, settlement, imperial enterprise and colonial "development"' but they seek to 'create or recreate an independent local identity [by] constructing or reconstructing alternative (alter/native) narratives'[4] (B&T 77). Thus novels as disparate as Australian Patrick White's *A Fringe of Leaves* (1976), Canadian Margaret Atwood's *Surfacing* (1973) and Barbadian George Lamming's *Natives of My Person* (1971) can all be seen to 'centre on the journey, rewriting the Conradian metaphor of the voyage into the heartland' (B&T 31). Both the eponymous protagonist of *i is a long memoried woman* (1983), *Starting the Flying Fish* (2005) and that of the title poem of *Sunris* (1996)[5] can be seen as epic journeyers, 'seekers' whose quests involve a re-encounter with, and ultimately a decentring of, European history and mythology, as they discover and reaffirm the multiple ancestries, alter/native narratives and indigenous traditions which are part of their identities. Nichols's description of the journey undertaken by the protagonist of 'sunris' as a 'journey towards self-discovery and self-naming' (*S* 4) is, in this sense, equally applicable to the protagonist of her earlier poem cycle.[6]

Nichols's interest in and treatment of mythology is important. In a similar way to Derek Walcott, she admits indebtedness to European myth, as well as recognizing the potentially damaging effects of Europe's myths on the black psyche. She acknowledges: 'Literature isn't a static thing. The myths of old were created by the poets of old and remain powerful sources of imagination, to be drawn on again and again. Odysseus in his rolling ship did a lot for mine as a child and I am grateful' (LN 102). However, she also argues:

> [Mythology] has created certain images and archetypes that have come down to us over the ages, and I have observed how destructive, however inadvertently, many of them have been to the black psyche. As children we grew up with the all-powerful male white God and the biblical associations of white with light and goodness, black with darkness and evil. We feasted on that whole world of Greek myths, European fairy-tales and legends, princes and princesses, Snowhites [*sic*] and Rapunzels. I'm interested in the psychological effects of this on black people even up to today, and how it functions in the minds of white people themselves . . . I think that white people have to be aware of this . . . and question it. I feel we also have to come up with new myths and other images that please us. (LN 101)

47

For Nichols, the key is to resist the notion of myth as static or as exclusively European; instead she asserts the need to 'keep on creating and reshaping' (LN 102). Liz Yorke makes a similar point when she argues that black poets (and lesbian poets)

> have played an important role in producing poetic revisionary mythologies. Their work has shown that [these] groups, however they are marginalised, may devise specific strategies of writing to break against, through, out of those essentialist definitions and mythic models which still oppress, still and subdue them.[7]

However, revisioning myth is not just the province of black and lesbian women poets but of contemporary women writers more widely.

It is also the project of Derek Walcott in *Omeros* (1990), one of the most important revisionings of European, classical myth by a Caribbean writer. As a male poet writing back to the Odysseus myth, Walcott might have been expected to recreate the male-centred, homosocial world of Homer's original epic poem. However, as Paula Burnett has argued:

> The representation of women in *Omeros* is also remarkably radical. Walcott revolutionises the patriarchal Western epic, with its militarist ethic and heroic action-men, to place at its centre the strong woman: principled, generous, courageous and tough. (PB 142)

Indeed, Burnett goes as far as to argue that:

> *Omeros* can be described in terms of *écriture féminine* in that its construction of gender contests patriarchal stereotypes, and this is as much to do with the representation of men as of women. Epic's gender convention of the active hero and passive heroine [just one permutation of what Cixous terms patriarchal binary oppositions] is inverted, its sexual politics revolutionised. (PB 142)

Walcott's concern not only to rewrite epic from a postcolonial or Caribbean perspective, but also to 're-map ... gender in his revolutionary epic' (PB 146), can therefore be seen as related to Nichols's revisionist project in her rewriting of the epic journeys of Caribbean literature from a woman-centred perspective in *i is* and 'sunris'.

Whereas *i is* is the most sustained revisioning of the many historical and literary accounts of slavery that neglect the gendered specificity of the slave woman's experience, 'sunris' is perhaps Nichols's fullest realization of the power of revisionist mythmaking. In this long poem, Nichols renegotiates woman's relationship to myth by having her protagonist re-appropriate indigenous mythologies and cultural icons in a Caribbean context.[8] Like the long memoried woman and the cari woman in *Starting the Flying Fish*, the protagonist of 'sunris' dialogues with mythological and historical figures from the region's past by means of spiritual and imaginative journeying, but the enabling device in 'sunris' is quite specific: the transformative power of Caribbean carnival, rather than the more diffuse sorcery and supernaturalism of *i is a long memoried woman*.

Alicia Suskin Ostriker argues that myths are 'large structures in which gendered images have always been embedded and suggest that revisionist mythmaking in women's poetry is a means of redefining both woman and culture' (AO 211). She suggests that women have traditionally been alienated from identification with mythic narratives because of their overwhelmingly male authorship and the sharply polarized and restricted gender roles for women in many European mythologies. Moreover, women writers have often been 'denied . . . the high literary status that myth confers . . . because they write "personally" or "confessionally" ' (AO 215). However, despite this, the use of myth is peculiarly attractive to many women writers since it is also 'quintessentially intimate material, the stuff of dream life, forbidden desire, inexplicable motivation – everything in the psyche that to rational consciousness is unreal, crazed or abominable' (AO 214). In other words, myth allows women writers to explore these areas of interest, without resort to a more transparently confessional mode, by 'inhabiting' officially sanctioned mythical personae; this also enables them to subvert such mythic narratives from within.

Speaking of major poetic works of revisionist myth published by American women poets since 1960, Ostriker points out:

> These poems generically assume the high literary status that myth confers and that women writers have often been denied . . . But in them the old stories are changed, changed utterly, by female knowledge of female experience, so that they can no longer stand as foundations of collective male fantasy or

as the pillars sustaining phallocentric 'high' culture. Instead, they are corrections; they are representations of what women find divine and demonic in themselves; they are retrieved images of what women have collectively and historically suffered; in some cases they are instructions for survival. (AO 214)

This also seems a productive way of speaking of Nichols's use of myth in her poetry, since it too is firmly grounded in a 'female knowledge of female experience' and 'knowledge throughout women's mythmaking is achieved through personal, intuitive, and subjective means'. Revisionist mythmaking involves reconnecting myth to a female subjectivity: re-centring woman in terms of narrative agency (woman as maker and breaker of myth) as well as re-evaluating and re-presenting her role in the myths themselves. It also often involves a reappraisal of female cultural practices, especially those traditionally feared or marginalized by phallocentric culture, such as magic, sorcery, and certain forms of spirituality. Clear examples of this can be found in Nichols's poetry. They include: 'Eve' and 'Configurations' in *Lazy Thoughts of a Lazy Woman*, and 'The Queen of Sheba . . .', 'Mnemosyne', 'Icons' and 'sunris' itself in *Sunris*.

This is part of what Adrienne Rich terms 'writing as re-vision' . . . the act of looking back, of seeing with fresh eyes, of entering an old text from a new critical direction'. She argues that revisioning 'is for woman more than a chapter in cultural history; it is an act of survival' (AO 235). Helene Cixous makes a similar point in 'The Laugh of Medusa', a polemical piece itself centrally concerned with the relationship between women's writing and myth, when she argues: 'If we women read them [myths] we read them otherwise'.

In 'Eve' and 'Icons' Nichols wryly turns to the biblical figure of Eve, concluding:

> Of all the women haunting
> the thin pages of the Bible . . .
> I would have to give it to Eve . . .
> – ingenuous Eve
> who not only came back with the apple
> but also with the eel of the first menses
> newly hatched. Coyly clasped.

(LTLW 14)

In this 'revisioning', Eve is reclaimed from phallocentric renderings of her merely as the precipitator of original sin; in Nichols's poem female sexuality, the cyclic rhythms and procreative potential of the female body are positively valued rather than seen as the marks of difference and shame. In a beautifully understated echo of the serpent in the tree who tempted Eve, her 'first menses' is described as an 'eel . . . newly hatched'. Although 'coyly clasped' in this poem, elsewhere in the collection it will be more explicitly celebrated as an integral part of womanhood. (See 'Ode to My Bleed', *LTLW* 24.)

In 'Icons' Nichols's focus is rather on the cultural politics of that most un-Caribbean and mythologically charged of fruits: the apple. The poem's opening images are of apples as 'English icons praised to the skies' (*S* 24), precious as jewels – and doubly so for being foreign: 'Everything foreign being better than local/ Or so it seemed as a child'. The poem then muses on why the poem's persona was 'hardly ever tempted/ To bite or ravish' (*S* 24), and ends with an image of her British 'apple-eating daughters' as Eves in reverse 'Two sun-starved Eves' 'drooling endlessly over the mango . . . making a meal of the old creation myth' (*S* 25). In both poems myth is revisioned in such a way that it is reconnected intimately to female experience and female subjectivity. The easy colloquialism of these and many other of Nichols's poems is important, for it 'modernizes what is ancient, making us see the contemporary relevance of the past. It also reduces the verbal glow that we are trained to associate with mythic material' (*AO* 236).

'Configurations' is a more complex reworking of the collective sexual fantasies and mythologies underpinning the encounter between Europe and Africa, a subject fellow Guyanese/black British poet David Dabydeen has also explored extensively in his poetry.[9] 'Configurations' uses the sexual encounter between the European colonizing male and a generic black woman as a metonym for a longer history of mythologizing and commodification of the black female body and the unequal exchange between colonizer and colonized. Nichols puns on the sexual connotations of the title – 'He gives her all the configurations/ of Europe' (*LTLW* 31) – but is also concerned to excavate a whole history of myths and misrepresentations: the second, more complex sense of 'configurations' in the poem. In a recent reading, Gina Wisker argues that 'Configurations':

> enacts and explodes the male coloniser's myths of the highly sexed Black woman, a dumb female Caliban over-awed by the white imperialist's stunning civilised gifts. The poem works by using a naïve point of view, exaggerating the achievements of the coloniser, a contemporary Columbus who conquers the girl, claiming the kudos of European civilization, including [ironically, an element capable of producing both energy and weapons of destruction] plutonium. In the exchange, she gives him all the white coloniser's fantasies of highly sexed, obedient native women. 'He does a Columbus' flinging himself on her shores. But the Anansi-wise Black woman mocks power in an initially exciting sexual act, making a 'stool of his head'. The double reading of stool (to sit on, faeces, excreta) shows her subtle triumph.[10]

Whilst the black woman commands control of the sexual act and does resemble the cunning cultural resistance of the West African trickster figure Anansi the spider god, it is possible to read the poem's ending as altogether more ambiguous. What Wisker fails to note is the importance of the 'golden stool' as a sacred artefact in Ghanaian culture, the ceremonial seat upon which the Ashanti king would sit, for one day only each year.[11] Indeed, in 'The Assertion' the fat black woman appropriates just such a 'golden stool' from the male elders and 'refuses to move . . . [saying] *This is my birthright'* (FBW 8). To 'mak[e] a golden stool of the empire/ of his head' (LTLW 31) thus suggests extraordinary reverence rather than disdain, although Wisker may be right to stress the woman's cunning and the possible irony of this most intimate form of reverence. The poem may even chart what Adrienne Rich calls 'an act of survival' (cited in AO 235).

One of the most illuminating of Ostriker's comments in relation to *i is,* is the recognition that 'to be great in our culture usually requires being big . . . If male poets write large, thoughtful poems while women write petite, emotional poems, the existence of book-length mythological poems by women on a literary landscape signifies trespass' (AO 223). One of her case studies is the American modernist poet Hilda Doolittle (H.D.) and her long poem, *Helen in Egypt* (1961). Ostriker argues that

The narrative of Helen in Egypt resembles that of traditional epic in that it pursues a journey ... Unlike the epic hero, however, she does not know her own goal in advance and must discover it through fluid and non-linear psychic processes which constitute her real adventure – meditation, memory, prayer, questioning, and associative weavings among 'the million personal things,/ things remembered, forgotten,/ remembered again, assembled/ and re-assembled in different order' (p. 289 – omitted from the accounts of Homer and all the subsequent poets. Also unlike the epic hero, her role is not to support but to 'unravel' and rewrite 'the already-written drama or script' (p. 231) of religion and history. (AO 224)

Much of this could also be applied to the form and content of *i is*, *Starting the Flying Fish* and 'sunris' which are also female epics in which the respective protagonists do 'not know [their] own goal[s] in advance and must discover it through fluid and non-linear psychic processes which constitute [their] real [journeys] – meditation, memory, prayer, questioning, and associative weavings'. Indeed, Nichols describes the protagonist of 'sunris' as 'always aware of the "unknown mission" in mind.While being open to the hedonist pull of carnival ... so that her dance becomes a dialectic, her spree a pilgrimage. In this act of reclaiming herself and the various strands of her heritage she engages with history and mythology' (S 5).

Like H.D.'s, Helen Nichols's protagonists are 'engaged in the recovery of her splintered selves, elements of [their] own character[s] and past[s] which have been "forgotten"' (AO 225). Both poets use revisionist techniques to address and redress the silences and omissions about gender of a previous, overwhelmingly male tradition of historical, literary and mythic narrative making. *Helen in Egypt* can be seen as the apotheosis of H.D.'s lifelong interest (both scholarly and creative) in the role of gender in classical mythology, a desire both to interrogate and to write herself into a tradition whose narratives and cultural authority were traditionally regarded as the province of the male poet only. Her intervention can also be seen as a significant response to the androcentrism of European literary modernism,[12] Nichols's *i is* can similarly be seen, in part, as a response to the male dominance of much early Caribbean literature and to the invisibility of gender in many historical and other narratives of slavery. Nichols's position has also been read as a challenge to the neglect of gender in more recent theoretical discourse.[13]

Nichols's concern to foreground gendered experience and her choice of a female protagonist for *i is* is thus crucial. Indeed, Nichols has commented that:

> In both my fiction and poetry, women characters figure strongly, for I am conscious that Caribbean female characters have largely been portrayed by men. But while exploring my female heritage does excite my imagination at a conscious level, writing is also very much an unconscious process . . . As the cycle of poems [*i is*] began to develop I was aware that I was dealing with my whole female history but I don't see my work as limited to women.   (HT 298)

More recently she has said in interview:

> I feel very multicultural as a writer, though Africa has always been the strongest spiritual strand for me . . . whenever I think of the ancestor, the ancestor is to me an African ancestor . . . an African woman. She may be the muse for me . . . And from her, I get that kind of strength, because she is the woman who has been, in history, negated and voiceless, but has persisted and flowered regardless.   (KD 138)

In its use of the journey motif, 'its poem-cycle structure and its merging of the particular and the universal, the concrete and the mythical', *i is a long memoried woman* is often seen 'as parallel in some ways to [fellow Caribbean poet, Kamau] Brathwaite's long trilogies': *The Arrivants*, *Mother Poem*, *Sun Poem* and *X-Self* (D&LW 368). 'This is especially true of parts of *The Arrivants* and *Mother Poem* which explore similar subject matter: African cultural legacies in the Caribbean, the role of Caribbean woman in relation to male histories, the geography and 'geopsyche'[14] of the Caribbean and how the landscape might be gendered in certain ways' (D&LW 168). Ironically, Nichols recalls how comparisons to Brathwaite's first trilogy militated against her finding a publisher for *i is*:

> When I began writing the cycle, I was very much aware that I was dealing with my whole female history, looking back at that, because we didn't have that perspective . . . in Caribbean literature. What's interesting is . . . some of the publishers who rejected it,

including Oxford University Press; one of the reasons they gave . . . was that this area or this journey, was covered by the poet Edward [Kamau] Brathwaite already . . . I was coming from a very female perspective, and . . . exploring the whole female psyche, so I couldn't see their rationale at all. (MB 18)

Nichols's comments signal just how far Anglophone Caribbean literature was still dominated by male writers in the late 1970s and how urgent was the project of opening up the literature not only to women's voices but to woman-centred explorations of identity, history and culture. The publication of Nichols's award-winning poem cycle, alongside the works of other Caribbean women writers such as Lorna Goodison, Erna Brodber, Olive Senior and Jamaica Kincaid in the early 1980s was thus highly significant. In this respect, *i is a long memoried woman* constitutes an important corrective to the androcentric bias of earlier literary explorations of this part of African Caribbean history.

I IS A LONG MEMORIED WOMAN

Nichols has described her long memoried woman as

something of a mythic figure. She breaks the slave stereotype of the dumb victim of circumstance. She is a woman of complex moods who articulates her situation with vision. Her spirit goes off wandering, meeting women from other cultures. She's a priestess figure and employs sorcery when necessary. (*LBT* 102)[15]

She is the nameless black woman uprooted from Africa and taken to the Caribbean. At times she was like an old black woman, at times she was like a young black woman. (R3F)

In this sense Nichols's poem cycle manifests one of the characteristics of black women's writing proposed by Lauretta Ngcobo. Ngcobo argues that 'Few of our writings are strictly personal in the subjective sense of encompassing individual exploits. Rather they reflect a collective subject, the common experience of Blackwomen reaching, reflecting and capturing different shades and depths and heights of moods' (LN 40).
However, this is not to suggest that Nichols constructs an essentialized black female subject in *i is*. Instead, the woman's

experiences shift between those which appear to take place in 'undifferentiated' (*DS* 124) times and spaces, and those which have very specific Caribbean referents and distinct historical and cultural markers. Thus Nichols includes references to the historical figure of Nanny of the Maroons and Maroon resistance against the British colonial authorities in Jamaica in the early 1700s. In the latter parts of the poem cycle, she also alludes to the Haitian Revolution of 1791 to 1804 which led to the establishment of the 'first black nation state in the New World, and the first country in which plantation slavery ended'.[16] As Patrick Williams has observed, 'This localising helps to offset an idealising tendency within the poems, the feeling that an essential Black femininity which persists regardless of circumstance is being posited'.[17]

Although physically confined on the plantation, the long memoried woman is able to transcend her situation, 'moving/ beyond/all/ boundaries' (*ILMW* 70) in various ways. She does this by dreaming (see 'One Dream'), by telling of oral traditional tales ('sweet tales of Dahomey') to the 'young ones' (*ILMW* 9) on the plantation, and most importantly by imaginatively and spiritually journeying through time and space. Such journeying allows her to keep 'true . . . to the wildness of my/ solitude and exile' (HC 68), whilst associating and communing with other women and other subjugated peoples, such as the Amerindians, the original indigenous population of the Caribbean, on a spiritual and mythical plane. In poems such as 'Drum Spell', 'Of Golden Gods', 'I Will Enter', 'Yemanji' and 'Nanny', her 'chameleon spirit/ take its exit' (*ILMW* 59) and she is able to travel back to her childhood in Africa and 'the Kingdom of Ancestors' (*ILMW* 26), across the continent of South America, back in time to its ancient civilizations and to 'genocides . . . all a prelude to my time' (*ILMW* 60).

However, the woman refuses to idealize. In 'Web of Kin' she admits: 'I come from a country of strong women/ Black Oak women who bleed slowly at/ the altars of their children/ because woman is supreme/ burden . . .' (*ILMW* 8) and responds: 'I will have nothing to do with it/ will pour it in the dust will set/ us free' (*ILMW* 9). The effect is to radically defamiliarize 'Mother Africa' and to remind us that a matrifocal society is not necessarily advantageous to or contiguous with a society in which women have extensive rights and freedoms. In this way Nichols's poetry can be seen to cross borders and boundaries, problematizing and collapsing simplistic binaries (for example, Africa is necessarily good, the Caribbean necessarily bad for the woman).

Significantly the woman's journeying, which is not just literal, but also a kind of cosmic wandering, an ability to psychically inhabit different spaces and times, is common to all Nichols's major female protagonists (notably the protagonist of 'sunris'). As Nichols says of her poem-cycle: 'It's a whole, for me, a whole psychic journey in which the woman manages to survive the harshness and the sense of loss and brutality because of the strength of her own vision, the power of her own vision and spirit' (R3F).

Ostriker notes how in Adrienne Rich's poem, 'The Mirror in Which Two Are Seen as One', 'A woman seeking her identity is like a woman attempting to give birth to herself' (*STL* 59). Birth images also abound in Nichols's poem cycle. In the early parts of *i is*, birth imagery is closely linked to the female body. In 'One Continent/ to Another' the violent rupture of a familiar way of life, the expulsion of the African into an enslaved existence in another continent, is figured in images of childbirth:

> Child of the middle passage womb
> Push
> Daughter of a vengeful chi
> She came
>   Into the new world
> Birth aching her pain
> From one continent/ to another
>
> Moaning
>
> Her belly cry sounding the wind
>
> (*ILMW* 5)

These rather abstract images rapidly give way to the concrete immediacy of the woman's memories of the 'Middle Passage':

> after fifty years
> she hasn't forgotten . . .

> how she had laid there
> in her own blood
> laid there in her own shit
>
> bleeding memories in the darkness
>
> how she stumbled onto the shore
> how the metals dragged her down
> how she thirsted . . .

(ILMW 5)

Later in the poem cycle, in 'New Birth', the woman's ability not merely to endure but to envisage life after the Middle Passage and to see it as a kind of rebirth – 'the Black Beginning' – links her to the kind of visionary creativity in a Caribbean context most famously espoused by Derek Walcott. Walcott's much quoted comment that 'Though there is nothing, there is everything to be made'[18] originally referred to his sense of the lack of a rooted tradition for the Caribbean artist, but it also carries this wider sense of a belief that the New World existence offers a unique opportunity for the creation of new forms and a new aesthetic. Indeed 'New Birth' captures exactly this sense of hope and new possibilities: the woman notes, in a very Walcottian phrase, 'the benediction of the sun' after 'the hurricane/ months had passed' (ILMW 70).

The 'new birth' of this poem refers, obliquely at first, to the woman's prophetic vision of a new order in which slavery will come to an end and colonial rule will be forced into decline: 'This Kingdom Will Not Reign/ Forever . . . plantations can perish/ lands turn barren' (ILMW 76). Destruction of the existing order will be the result of both elemental forces and human agency, as 'This Kingdom' makes clear:

> And we
> The rage growing
> Like the chiggers
> In our feet
>
> Can wait
> Or
> Take our freedom
>
> Whatever happens

(ILMW 76–7)

Thus the woman puts her hope in slave uprising, rebellion and revolt, epitomized for her by the guerrilla warfare waged against the British colonial authorities in Jamaica by Nanny and the Maroons, and the slave uprising led by Toussaint l'Ouverture which paved the way for the revolutionary struggle which led to the successful overthrow of slavery and the establishment of an independent state in San Domingo (now known as Haiti). Nichols has spoken of the crucial need to recuperate this history and make it more visible to Caribbean people:

> When we were learning history, we didn't learn much about the slave rebellions. [Yet] This was a part of the struggle of Caribbean people. They had constant rebellions. It doesn't matter how much inner growth and inner freedom we feel if in reality we are still enslaved. (R3F)

'One Continent/ To Another' is structured around a series of oppositions, the most central of which is the startling juxtaposition of life and death, sterility and fecundity, ends and beginnings. The woman is not 'prepared' for 'the utter/ rawness of life everywhere', having 'imagined this new world to be – / bereft of fecundity'. Importantly 'being born a woman/ she moved again/ knew it was the Black Beginning/ though everything said it was/ the end'. All she has is memory and 'the soft wet forest/ between her thighs' (*ILMW* 6), the sign of hopefulness but also of threat. As fellow Caribbean poet Marlene Nourbese Phillips has usefully observed:

> The black woman comes to the New World with only the body . . . And that most precious of resources – the space. Between . . . The space between the black woman's legs becomes *The place*. Site of oppression – vital to the cultivation and continuation of the outer space in a designated form – the plantation machine. Harness the use value of the inner space to the use value of the outer space so that the inner space becomes open to all and sundry. Becomes, in fact, a public space. A thoroughfare. The 'black magic' of the white man's pleasure, the 'bag o'sugar down dey' of the black man's release. And the space through which new slaves would issue forth . . . For the black woman, place and space come together in the New World as never before. Or since.[19]

Indeed, Nichols's poem cycle is finely attuned to the specific experiences of the African *woman* under slavery, the ways in which her experiences differed from those of other slaves and from those of other women. In 'We the Women' the woman finds community amongst fellow slave women. Despite the slave woman's central importance to the sexual and reproductive life of the plantation economy, 'women were [still] valued more as labor units than childbearers':

> pregnant women or mothers with families ... were subjected to the same brutality as were men [and] it was only after the abolition of the slave trade in 1807 that the planters were forced to introduce measures to protect pregnant women to ensure the continuation of an adequate labor supply.   (SC 9)

Although she is not yet pregnant herself, the woman notes how invisible she is and how seemingly dispensable is her life:

> ... we the women
> whose praises go unsung
> whose voices go unheard
> whose deaths they sweep aside
> as easy as dead leaves

(ILMW 12)

In the next poem, 'Waterpot' the woman responds to the dehumanizing treatment of the slaves by the overseer ('The daily going out/ and coming in/ always being hurried/ along/ like like ... cattle', *ILMW* 13) and the desexing effect of the fieldwork which she is forced to undertake. She tries:

> hard to walk
> like a woman
> she tried very hard
> pulling herself erect ...
> pulling herself together
> holding herself like royal cane

(ILMW 13)

Against the 'sneer[ing]' of the overseer, she observes the dignity of a fellow slave woman in an image which reveals a spontaneous and unforced beauty:

> O but look
> There's a waterpot growing
> From her head

(ILMW 14)

This ability to see anew and to give dignity to the specific, the local, as a thing of beauty and grace (rather than the general, the European) is also a recurrent concern of Caribbean poets, most notably that of Derek Walcott.[20]

'Ala' describes the punishment of a 'rebel' slave woman who has killed her baby rather than see it live a life of slavery, 'sending the little-new-born/ soul winging its way back/ to Africa – free' (*ILMW* 23).[21] As Cudjoe notes:

> the female slave, it would seem, presented a challenge to the absolute power of the slave master and mistress which could be kept in check only by physical control (and subsequent humiliation) of the female slave ... an uncontrollable slave was an unmitigated threat against the system that was sure to lead to its downfall. In their aggressive and uncontrollable behaviour toward the slave master and mistress, slave women presented a challenge to the slave system that was as persistent as it was pervasive. (SC 8)

Although in this particular poem, the women appear to do little other than 'sing and weep/ as we work', invoking the female deity Ala to admit the woman 'to the pocket/ of your womb' (*ILMW* 24), they are still resistant subjects. Their resistance, crucially, is a *cultural* resistance to slavery and to the authority of the slave master and mistress, one which, though not as dramatic as the numerous slave uprisings of the 1700s and 1800s, was still crucial in enabling individuals to psychically and culturally survive the slave experience. Indeed:

> Women were in the vanguard of the cultural resistance to slavery which helped individuals survive the slave experience. Their important contribution to the 'private' life of slaves – the reconstitution of the family and the building of a viable black community life – ... [was a] cultural strength ... which helped women to resist the system in their more 'public' lives as workers.[22]

This is the significance of the protagonist's memories and her spiritual invocations to the African female deities Ala, Asaase Yaa, and Yemanji, and the male god Ogun (see 'Ala', 'Among the Canes', 'Yemanji', 'Time of Ogun/Mambu'). Through them and the transmission of other aspects of oral traditional culture from Africa, she helps to keep alive African cultural practices, belief systems and language in resistance to the imposed

European practices, beliefs and language. Such oral traditional resources include the 'sweet tales of Dahomey' which the long memoried woman 'feeds' the 'young ones' (*ILMW* 9), the women's worksongs in the fields (see 'We the Women', *ILMW* 12) and the allusions to the figure of Anansi, West African/ Caribbean folkloric spider-king/man (see 'Like Anansi', *ILMW* 66–7).

Her use of African language is particularly significant. European slave owners routinely forbade the use of African languages by the slaves on their plantations, and even went as far as deliberately selecting slaves from different tribal and/or language groups, in order to minimize the chances of slave insurrection. Kamau Brathwaite has argued that this proscription of African languages by the colonial powers led to the 'submergence of this imported language'. Its status, like that of its speakers, was deemed to be 'inferior'. However, its submerged nature also

> served an interesting intercultural purpose, because although people continued to speak English as it was spoken in Elizabethan times and on through the Romantic and Victorian ages, that English was, nonetheless, still being influenced by the underground language, the submerged language that the slaves had brought. And that underground language was itself constantly transforming itself into new forms. It was moving from a purely African form to a form which was African but which was adapted to the new environment and adapted to the cultural imperative of the European languages. And it was influencing the way in which the English, French, Dutch, and Spaniards spoke their own language. So there was a very complex process taking place, which is now beginning to surface in our literature.[23]

In 'Without Song' the woman notes with despair how:

> The faces of the children
> Are small and stricken and black
> They have fallen
> Into exile
> Moving without song
> Or prayer
>
> ... They have fallen
> into silence

> uttering no cry
> laying no blame

(ILMW 25)

Her words echo Psalm 137 unconsciously, or perhaps deliberately, as she laments her people's exiled state. Silence and inactivity seem to be the alternative to cultural resistance, a kind of living death. However, these lines pull in several directions as what the woman describes (a living death) is contradicted by what her words inscribe (the possibility of resistance).[24] Yet still the woman wonders whether

> Maybe the thing is to forget
> To forget and be blind
> On this little sugar island
>
> To forget the Kingdom of Ancestors
> The washing of throats with palm wine

(ILMW 26)

The fragility of memory and the vulnerability of the communal histories carried to the Caribbean by African slaves are felt all too palpably in this poem. Not only is the retention and retelling of these narratives in the Caribbean crucial, but also women have traditionally played a significant role in keeping such traditions alive, as Evelyn O'Callaghan notes (EO 7) The role of creole or nation language, as a linguistic form emerging in the Caribbean from the contact between different African language groups and the European, is important in this context. This is dramatically demonstrated in poems such as 'I Coming Back' and 'Hi De Buckras Hi!':[25]

> In the fields cultural defiance was expressed through language and song . . . Women field hands were experts in the use of rich creole language which, with its double entendres and satire, was frequently employed as subtle abuse of whites. Through such channels women helped to generate and sustain the general spirit of resistance.[26]

Indeed, the notion that female slaves were necessarily powerless and passive in their enslavement is thoroughly deconstructed throughout *i is*. In poems such as 'Nimbus', 'Night is Her Robe', 'Love Act', 'Skin Teeth', 'I Coming Back', 'Wind a

Change' and 'This Kingdom' Nichols stresses the significance of the female slaves' acts of resistance, however small or subtle, as well as a longer tradition of black female resistance, in poems such as 'The Return' and 'Nanny'. In 'I Coming Back' the long memoried woman imagines returning from the dead to exact revenge on her master ('Massa'), haunting and taunting him in various forms:

> Mistress of the underworld
> I coming back . . .
>
> Dog howling outside
> Yuh window
> I coming back
>
> Ball-a-fire
> And skinless higue[27]
> I coming back

$$(ILMW\ 42)$$

In 'Hi De Buckras Hi!' the long memoried woman targets her vengeance more specifically at the (white) 'buckra woman' and 'buckra man' 'from cold countree' (*ILMW* 43–4). Not only is the fragility and delicate constitution of the buckra woman ridiculed, but she is reviled for her 'airs and graces' and obliviousness to the reality of the slaves' lives:

> Being helped from carriages
> Being lifted over ditches
> Floating by white and pale
> Not even looking
> Not even seeing
> The pain and rage and black despair

$$(ILMW\ 43)$$

Similarly, the 'buckra man' is ridiculed for having 'pluck-chicken skin' and dressing 'fancee'; he is seen as equally vulnerable to the slave woman's sorcery. Nichols has referred to this poem as illustrating the wider subversive practices amongst slaves of 'composing songs that would mock the masters and the mistresses . . . behind the slave owner's back . . . poking fun at the slave master through mocking his language and telling stories in which he, the slave, was the one who came out a winner' (R3F). However, the poem is interesting in other ways. Paula Burnett notes that slave songs were the Caribbean's first poems.[28] In making use of indigenous forms, the improvised song and obeah spells in this poem, Nichols not only ensures historical authenticity but also effectively undermines the authority of European textual accounts and narratives of slavery.

Nichols has spoken of 'magic and the supernatural [as] a very strong part of Caribbean life, not just of African life' (R3F). In an early poem, 'Twentieth Century Witch Chant'[29] the poetic persona rhythmically casts her spell:

> Resurrect the ashes of the women burnt as witches
> Resurrect the ashes/ mould the cinders
> Stir the cauldron/ resurrect those witches . . .
> Resurrect
> Resurrect
> Resurrect
> And as for the boys playing with their power toys
> Entoad them all

As Gina Wisker notes, the poem calls 'on an entourage of historical women of strength, prophetesses and witches, who have been hidden and denied . . . demand[ing] a re-empowerment and resurrection of silenced and marginalised women of power'.[30] Elsewhere in her poetry, Nichols 'returns magic to the ordinary, reinvests the powers of women in the everyday world' (GWW 114):

> My mother had more magic
> In her thumb
> Than the length and breadth
> Of any magician
>
> Weaving incredible stories
> Around the dark-green senna brew
> Just to make us slake
> The ritual Sunday purgative
>
> Knowing when to place a cochineal poultice
> On a fevered forehead
> Knowing how to measure a belly's symmetry
> Kneading the narah pains[31] away . . .
>
> ('Abra-Cadabra', *LTLW* 29)

Magic, for Nichols, is broadly defined but is almost invariably the province of women.

Nichols has described how in *i is* 'The woman uses magic and sorcery, the supernatural, as conscious acts to help her in her survival' (R3F). The third part of the poem cycle is entitled 'Sorcery' and is centrally concerned with these indigenous cultural practices, which, as Nichols signals, were (and are) African legacies, brought to the Caribbean by the slave population. They therefore take on a particular significance as an alter/native resource and source of resistance to the European. In 'Nimbus' the woman is pictured

> sitting in the shadows
> countering darkness
> with darkness
> fingers caught in the rhythmic
> braiding of her
> hair

(*ILMW* 45)

as a nimbus, or cloud-like halo, grows sinisterly from her. Her 'laughter/ soft and harsh' (*ILMW* 45) is externally focalized, as though overheard by the plantation owner and his wife.

In the following poem, 'Night is Her Robe', she is seen

> gathering strange weeds
> wild root
> leaves with the property
> both to harm and to heal . . .
> with all the care
> of a herbalist

(*ILMW* 46)

This duality of purpose, for good or for evil, is characteristic of obeah practices more generally in the Caribbean. Indeed, to define obeah simply as a form of sorcery which is evil in intent is reductive and misleading. Obeah is, as Nichols notes, an important African cultural retention in the Caribbean. It needs to be seen as part of a complex matrix of women-centred cultural activities which range from herbalism at one end of the spectrum to a belief that it is possible to control the actions of others, to make someone love you, to bring sickness, even death. In her study of West Indian women's fiction, *Woman Version*, Evelyn O' Callaghan cites Carolyn Cooper's recognition that 'a revalorization of such "discredited knowledge" – in the sense of the term as used by Toni Morrison . . . is a major project in the female-centred fictions of [Caribbean women writers such as Sylvia Wynter, Erna Brodber and Paule Marshall]'. 'Reappropriation of what Cooper terms "devalued folk-wisdom" – that body of subterranean knowledge that is often associated with the silenced language of women and the "primitiveness" of orally transmitted knowledge . . . – is important to the recuperation of identity for the female in these works' (EO 6–7). It would seem to be equally important in Nichols's poem cycle.

Obeah beliefs intersect with a rich mythical and supernatural strain in the Caribbean and often take quite specific forms. Thus, in 'Kanaima Jungle', the woman is 'ensnared/ by jungle' which she suspects has been supernaturally orchestrated to trap or slow her down. 'Kanaima' is a specifically Guyanese term which refers to an evil force which may also take physical forms. In her notes to *Sunris*, Nichols describes Kanaima as the 'Amerindian figure of death. Also the spirit of vengeance' (S 83). Nichols has also spoken elsewhere of the intimate relationship between the Guyanese interior and its indigenous myths and folklore in ways which illuminate this section of the poem cycle (see HT 297).

In 'Old Magic', as in 'Skin Teeth', the woman mentally addresses the slave owner and warns that '[s]he isn't what/ [s]he seem' (*ILMW* 32):

> She . . .
> The curse you think
> You leave behind
>
> The woman made young
> With old magic
>
> The one you going
> Sleep with
>
> The one you going
> Think is kind

> (*ILMW* 47)

In 'Loveact' the woman uses her sexuality subversively in order to gain valuable access to the master's house and his family for her 'sorcery'. 'Soon she is the fuel/ That keep them all going' (*ILMW* 48), as she becomes sexual partner to the master, wet nurse to the children, and rids his wife of the necessity of participating in 'the loveact'. The master

> ... want to tower above her
> want to raise her ebony
> haunches and when she does
> he thinks she can be trusted
> and drinks her in ...
>
> But time pass/es
>
> Her sorcery cut them
> Like a whip
>
> She ride her triumph
> And slowly stir the hate
> Of poison in.

(ILMW 48–9)

The images of nurturing and feeding in this poem are treacherously reconfigured by the final lines, 'slowly stir the hate/ of poison in' and it is the woman, not the master, who metaphorically commands the 'whip'. The smile, which is interpreted by the master as the sign of her submission and compliance, is equally treacherous as the prologue had prophesied ('from dih/ treacherous/ calm of mih/ smile' (*ILMW* 3), for it refers to the false smile in which the skin is unnaturally tightly drawn over the teeth. As the woman reminds the master:

> know that I smile
> know that I bend
> only the better
> to rise and strike
> again

(ILMW 50)

Nichols has spoken about 'Skin Teeth' in terms of undermining the white stereotype of the servile, 'always smiling slave': 'They don't know that behind that smile, or behind that servility is a plotting mind. As they say . . . people stoop to conquer; it's that kind of survival technique that people who are dispossessed and who don't have the power use and ['Skin Teeth'] illustrates this' (R3F).

Indeed, the spirit of rebellion and the recognition that 'all revolutions are rooted in dreams' (*ILMW* 10) runs throughout the poem cycle as an organizing motif. It is present from the prologue and 'Days that Fell' onwards but most visible in later poems such as 'Dark Sign', 'Blow Winds Blow', 'Wind a Change' and '. . . And Toussaint'. Whereas in early poems such as 'Eulogy', 'Taint', 'Sunshine' and 'Without Song' the woman is, in Nichols's words, 'weighed down and she's lamenting about slavery, a woman uprooted . . . gradually she begins to question things to herself, she begins to employ her own woman magic and power to strengthen herself' (RF3).

One of the major turning points in the cycle is 'Your Blessing'. In the earlier 'Sacred Flame' the woman refers to herself as 'armed only with/ my mother's smile', her many selves exiled and dispersed. 'I must be forever gathering/ my life together like scattered beads' (*ILMW* 19). In 'Your Blessing', newly pregnant and 'tainted with guilt and/ exile.burden with child and maim . . . severed by ocean and/ longing' (*ILMW* 53), she finds the strength to call for her mother's blessing:

> Heal me with the power of your blackness
>
> Cover me
> Heal me
> Shield me . . .
>
> Uplift me
> Instruct me
> Reclothe me
>
> With the power of your blessings

> (*ILMW* 53)

'Torn from their mothers and [African] mother culture'[32] the long memoried woman, like Sethe in Toni Morrison's *Beloved*, can only reconnect with the nurturing, healing figure of the mother imaginatively or spiritually. Invocations to female deities (as in 'Ala', *ILMW* 23–4 and 'Yemanji', *ILMW* 64), calls to mother figures (as in 'Your Blessing and 'Sacred Flame', *ILMW* 19–20) and the acknowledgement of the centrality of female community to women's lives (as in 'Drum-Spell, *ILMW* 28–30) recur throughout Nichols's poetry and are characteristic of the woman-centredness of Caribbean women's writing more widely.

Sexuality features in a number of poems in the cycle, most famously in the much-anthologized 'Sugar Cane'. Kwame Dawes's term 'the erotics of surprise' is a useful one in this context. Nichols has spoken of sugar cane as

> the crop responsible for bringing slavery to the Caribbean, so I see so much when I see sugar cane. I also see great spiritual endurance and strength. For me, sugar cane is a symbol of Caribbean history, first and foremost, but it also has . . . little erotic overtones because of the shape of the sugar cane, in the sweetness of the juice . . . and all these things come together and make it a 'back home' symbol. (*PGN*)

Nichols describes sugar cane as a 'sweet crop with a bitter history . . . bitter because of the enormous suffering [of] the early Amerindians, who were almost wiped out through having to cultivate sugar cane . . . and then the African slaves who suffered a whole lot of degradation and oppression'. She describes how sugar cane was made into 'a very human male figure . . . in this particular poem because it is a slave woman relating to sugar cane' (*PGN*). She sees sugar cane

> as oppressive at one level because she has to exert such hard physical labour to cultivate [it], but on another level she sees sugar cane as a victim because in the same way that the slaves and she has her sweat wrung out of her, so the cane has his sugar wrung out of him. So she attributes . . . very human characteristics to sugar cane – like shivering from ague and suffering from belly work, which are very . . . 'back home' ailments. (*PGN*)

'Sugar Cane' has also attracted interest due to its layout on the page.[33] Nichols herself has spoken of the 'importance of the shape of that particular poem . . . I wanted to capture the actual length of sugar cane so I wrote it out in that elongated way' (*PGN*).

After sexual liaisons with a fellow slave in 'I Go to Meet Him' ('kin of my skin you are' [*ILMW* 37]) and with the white

slave master in 'Love Act', the long memoried woman finally
gives birth to her 'tainted/ perfect child' in 'In My Name'
(*ILMW* 56). Water, one of the recurrent motifs of this poem
cycle and a favoured metaphor in women's writing, functions
in this poem both as an agent of cleansing and reconnection
with Africa: 'with my tears/ I've pooled the Niger' and of
death . . . 'now my sweet one it is for you to swim' (*ILMW* 57).

The poems which follow are central to the woman's journeying. In 'The Wandering' she invokes all the spirits of the
natural world to be 'at one with me' (*ILMW* 58). Carolyn
Cooper has argued that 'the use of the trope of spirit
possession [is] metaphorical of the recovery of African cultural
values in the black diaspora' (EO 6). However, Nichols's
concern with the recovery of the ancestors is much wider in its
reach. In interview she has commented that she feels 'a kinship
with the Amerindian people of Guyana, for example, their
myths and legends . . . The Guyana hinterland is very much in
my psyche so that part of me feels a bit South American and
the incredible destruction of the Aztec/Inca civilisation also
informs our heritage' (LN 96).

Such comments are directly relevant to 'Of Golden Gods' in
which the 'chameleon spirit' (*ILMW* 59) of the woman 'take its
exit' and ranges across the South American continent:

> . . . up past the Inca ruins
> and back again
> drifting onto Mexican plains
> the crumbling of golden gods
> and Aztec rites
> speak for themselves
> that, and before, the
> genocides –
> all a prelude to my time.

(ILMW 59–60)

In 'I Will Enter', the woman 'allows her spirit to walk and meet
women from other cultures and she was merging with the
female spirits from other worlds. She bonds with a woman
from the South American continent, that the indigenous
woman would [have] gone through a similar experience of
being colonized' (R3F):

Your tongue is silent
Your eyes speak of an
Ancient weariness
I too have known
Memory is written in each crumpled fold
You can still remember
How they pitted gun against arrow
Steel against stillness

(ILMW 62)

In 'Yemanji' and 'The Return' (as well as in the later 'Nanny'), the woman looks for guidance from other female figures: the Nigerian Yoruba deity Yemanji, and the Jamaican folk heroine and historical figure Nanny of the Maroons. Yemanji (or Yemanja or Yemoja) is also the subject of Nichols's 'On the Eve of the Summer Solstice' (*S* 46–7) and is mentioned in 'sunris' (*S* 73). Moreover, she is the subject of poems by other black women writers such as Audre Lorde (see, for example, 'The Winds of Orisha'[34]) and Jamaican poet Olive Senior (see 'Yemoja'[35]). In her note to *Sunris*, Nichols describes Yemanja as 'The ultimate symbol of motherhood. Orisha of the river and the ocean. She is said to have attained greater proportions since her "middle passage" crossing to the New World and is widely worshipped, especially in Brazil [the setting for "On the Eve of the Summer Solstice"]' (*ILMW* 86). It is said that from her breasts the rivers flow and this is the significance of the long memoried woman's encounter with her by the riverside, as well as the call to Yemanja by the protagonist of 'sunris' to 'cool me down ... bathe my face in your river' (*S* 73). In drawing upon such alter/native mythic resources, Nichols decentres European myth whilst foregrounding the female principle at work in her cycle. Olive Senior has spoken of similar aims in certain of her poems:

I wrote the poem 'Mystery' because I was really thrilled to discover Yoruba culture ... because, of course, I grew up learning a lot about Greek and Roman myths – it was part of the curriculum. The African Orishas are much more fascinating, because ... they are still alive. Their histories and personalities are just as interesting ... but we have never been told anything about them'. (KD 82–3).

In 'The Return' and 'Nanny', the woman looks to Nanny and identifies her as a priestess figure, combining impressive leadership and obeah powers:

> Ashanti Priestess
> and giver of charms
> earth substance woman
> of science
> and black fire magic
>
> Maroonic woman
> Of courage and blue mountain rises
>
> ... your voice giving
> sound to the Abeng
>
> (*ILMW* 72)

The reference to Abeng is to Nanny's instrument of communication, a conch shell 'whose womb-like shape has given it feminine connotations'.[36] It was 'blown both by plantations overseers to call slaves to work, and by the Maroon armies to mobilise resistance'[37] and has become a symbol of maroon rebellion and resistance in Jamaica.

'Like Anansi' stands out as an interesting exception here as the trickster spider god of West African origin is usually associated with a male principle. However, in Nichols's poem the woman likens herself to the 'Ashanti spider/ woman-keeper/ of dreamer', his 'calm ... cunning' and survival instinct. She also encounters a mysterious presence, Amerindian in appearance, who is 'not at all/ what I was expecting' (*ILMW* 66). Anansi-like, we are unsure if this is Nanny or even Anansi himself in disguise.

The following poems, 'Blow Winds Blow', 'This Kingdom', 'Wind a Change', 'Time of Ogun/Mambu', 'Omen' and '... And Toussaint', chart mounting tension and ill omens which precede the overthrow of the 'kingdom' of the plantocracy. This takes place on two fronts: on the slave plantations, led notably by Toussaint l'Ouverture, and in the form of guerrilla warfare waged on the colonial centres from the remote, mountainous interior by Nanny and the Maroons. Ogun is another of the gods in the 'Yoruba pantheon', described by Nichols in her notes to *Sunris* as 'god of war. Symbols include

73

the knife, iron and anvil. He is the father of metamorphosis; the patron of those who work in metal, wood and leather' (*S* 85). In Nichols's poem cycle his warlike associations are obviously most relevant; however, in other Caribbean poems, such as Kamau Brathwaite's 'Ogun' in *The Arrivants*,[38] his role as patron saint of those who work in wood is to the fore, as the poem deals with a Caribbean carpenter.

After the violence and bloodshed charted in '... And Toussaint', the long memoried woman encounters, in 'I Cross Myself', 'bodies ... quite headless ... Under the scarlet blossoms of the poincianas' (*ILMW* 85). As Nichols explains: 'She almost regrets that it had to come to this, that blood had to be shed for the slaves to be free' (R3F) and turns her energies to rites of purification and 'clos[ing] the eyes of the children with my lips/ I lead them quickly away' (*ILMW* 85).

In the penultimate poem of the cycle, 'Holding My Beads', the woman finally finds a kind of peace as she realizes that her journey has not been in search of

> privilege or pity reverence or safety
> $\qquad$ but
> the power to be what I am/ a woman
> charting my own futures/ a woman
> holding my beads in my hand

(ILMW 86)

The image of the beads in this poem is a complex one. It combines references to trade and colonialism (the beads given to the indigenous peoples by Columbus and the early colonizers); to religious observance and the ritualized re-memory which is found in both European and African traditions (the rosary, reading one's beads); and to femininity.[39] Nichols's comment in interview that 'In anything I do in life I feel that people should grow and come to terms with themselves, respect themselves and win' (R3F) illuminates 'Holding My Beads'. As she suggests: 'At the beginning of the book she is weighed down and she's lamenting about slavery, a woman uprooted. But gradually she begins to question things to herself, she begins to employ her own woman magic and power to strengthen herself. So she develops as a character' (R3F).

In the much-quoted epilogue to *ILMW*, the woman reflects on the extent of her journeying and the constant potential for regrowth and the creation of new forms in the New World, as symbolized by the emergence of nation language, the creole 'tongue':

> I have crossed an ocean
> I have lost my tongue
> from the root of the old
> one
> A new one has sprung

(ILMW 87)

It is, as Carole Boyce Davies has argued, 'an "epilogue" which nevertheless opens',[40] as much of a beginning as an ending. As such, Nichols' epic poem cycle ends with the recognition that 'diasporas are also potentially the sites of hope and new beginnings' (AB 193).

4

Epic Journeying II: 'sunris'

The poem 'sunris' is inspired by what Nichols terms the 'wit, wordplay, bravado and gusto' (*S* 18) of calypso and the spirit of carnival more generally. In her introduction to the collection, Nichols describes the poem, like *i is a long memoried woman* before it, as a poem of female journeying:

> In my 'sunris' poem, a woman makes a journey towards self-discovery and self-naming, through carnival ... In this act of reclaiming herself and the various strands of her heritage she engages with history and mythology and like the calypsonian sometimes resorts to verbal self-inflation to make her voice heard, 'I think this time I go make history'. (*S* 5)

In interview Nichols has described the journey as a kind of 'pilgrimage':

> it is a pilgrimage because ... carnival is very much linked up to the whole religious Christian festival of Lent ... coming just before that and ending on the Tuesday just before Ash Wednesday, the religious significance is implicit in it, and the woman is making ... a sacred journey through carnival, it's a journey towards a new self-discovery, a discovery of ... her mythic self. It's ... a healing reclamation also of her different cultural and racial strands. (*WH*)

In choosing carnival as the vehicle for her protagonist's journey of 'self-discovery and self-naming' (*S* 5), Nichols locates her poem within a distinctive Caribbean literary tradition of texts inspired by a carnival aesthetic and the cultural practices specific to Caribbean carnival, namely the calypso.[1]

The poem shifts between the present of making mas (actively taking part in carnival) and the historical and mythical past of the Caribbean. Carnival is the perfect vehicle for the protagonist's encounter with historical figures such as Montezuma, Cortez, Columbus and supernatural entities such as the Guyanese/Amerindian Kanaima and Papa Bois,[2] since its aesthetic is by definition radically transformative: 'playing mas' involves metamorphosis – mas players *become* the role they are playing for the duration of carnival. Moreover carnival, from its very first beginnings, has been no respecter of social and racial hierarchies; indeed, it overturns and disrupts them. In mas, black can become white and vice versa, the ordinary woman can become a queen or a goddess, one can take on the form of an animal, a mythic figure or a deity. As fellow Guyanese writer Pauline Melville usefully comments:

> I enjoy carnival because anybody can take on any form: an Egyptian goddess; a Mabaruma warrior; a sultan; a demon; a frog. Race, gender, class, species and divinity are all in the melting-pot ... Carnival plays with identity. It is masquerade where disguise is the only truth ... Death comes in the guise of uniformity, mono-cultural purity, the externals of the state as opposed to the riot of the imagination.[3]

The origins of Caribbean carnival are disputed, with some commentators arguing that it started out as the preserve of the French Creole upper classes in pre-Emancipation Trinidad; others, such as Trinidadian dramatist Errol Hill, argue that its appropriation by the freed blacks in the post-emancipation period marks its real beginnings and that it developed as a vehicle of ritualized resistance or rebellion against colonial power. Critics such as Hill and Brathwaite argue that carnival's definitive practices, such as calypso, have West African origins, a line which Nichols also takes (*S* 4).

It has been argued that early carnival functioned primarily as an officially sanctioned 'safety-valve' or 'mechanism of social release' (David Cuffy, cited in *S* 2) for the slave population. However, its history has been one of censorship and repression, as Nichols notes (*S* 2). She recalls how, even in her own childhood in Guyana in the 1950s, considerable disapprobation and opposition were directed at 'carnival, steel pan, calypso, in fact anything that came from the ordinary folk including the Creole language' (*S* 4) by the colonial powers and sectors of the upper and middle classes. This is one of the reasons why the Caribbean writer's conscious use of creole, her drawing upon oral traditions and other alter/native forms deriving from the 'folk', are so important.

In his essay 'Nation Language' Kamau Brathwaite argues that it is precisely such a history of creole or nation language being proscribed by the white overseer and denied official status, that pushed it underground and gave it what he terms a uniquely 'submerged nature'.[4] This, for Brathwaite, is the key to creole's subversive political potential. Similarly, by allowing the symbolic enaction of inversions of the sacred and the profane and other modes of status reversal, so central to Bakhtin's concept of the carnivalesque, carnival, and particularly calypso, facilitated satirical comment and mockery of those occupying the traditional bases of authority in church and colonial government.[5] As David Cuffy notes, the freedoms of carnival and the 'journey of freedom' which it enacts make 'Trinidad carnival . . . a deeply resonant anniversary from the bondage of colonial slavery' (cited in S 2). Indeed, the protagonist of 'sunris' declares herself to be 'Symbol of the emancipated woman' (S 53). Despite mass sponsorship, increasing commercialization and the indisputable investment of the tourist industry in Trinidad's annual carnival, 'playing mas' still retains something of this subversive, rebellious, transformative quality, as Nichols demonstrates in 'sunris'.

The publication of the individual collections which comprise Kamau Brathwaite's poetic trilogy, *The Arrivants*, in the late 1960s and early 1970s, marked a radical breakthrough in Caribbean poetry by demonstrating that the thematic, rhythmic and formal resources of a wide range of black (including Caribbean) musical forms could be utilized in poetic form. Although an American and African-American tradition of closely aligning speech and song, music and poetry already existed, arguably no Caribbean writer had so fully realized the poetic possibilities of exploring specifically Caribbean forms such as carnival and its music: calypso and steel pan, as well as musical forms such as mento, ska and reggae.

Since then a wide range of Caribbean texts has appeared which continue to explore carnival, steel pan and calypso.[6] Asked about 'the impact of reggae or calypso on [her] work and what other musical styles [she is] drawn to', Nichols has said: 'music has always been a big part of my work. Even in simple poems, that musical awareness, and awareness of sound and the way words sound is very much in my head when I am writing' (KD 146). In the same interview and in her introduction to *Sunris* (S 2–3), she recalls the role of music in her childhood:

> I grew up with a lot of music like most people in the Caribbean. There was woman who lived next door to us [in] . . . Georgetown . . . All hours of the day she'd be blaring out the latest Sparrow calypsos, so you'd be hearing 'Dove and Pigeon' and all these kinds of things.[7] So you grew up with all these rhythms, especially calypso, in your head, which I loved as a child. She could play her music whole day as far as I was concerned. It just livened up things whenever she put on her music. And then on the radio you would be hearing music. At weddings and so on, you would be getting some of the Queh Queh ceremonies . . . you had the Queh Queh night where they hid the bride and the women would be singing lots of bawdy songs and they would eventually go and find the bride. So all these old songs . . . we grew up with. Some were plain folk songs, but most of them had the sexual . . . the calypso, suggestiveness. I loved that . . . (KD 145)

> [Calypso] is the music of my childhood through which we got the news and scandals of the day; love and celebration, crime and tragedy, fantasy, politics and philosophy; in fact all of human experience and all in the people's language. (S 3)

Nichols describes 'sunris' as 'a long poem about a woman going through carnival and being transformed by it. And that . . . is directly linked to steel pan and calypsos – that influence. So . . . [in 'sunris'] I am trying to keep up that kind of [calypso] rhythm all the way through' (KD 145–6). The poem traces the woman's progress from the opening morning of carnival, J'Ouvert Morning, through to 'dih carnival straights' (S 72), the final stretch of the annual road march at which each mas band is judged and a carnival king and queen announced, and carnival's end on Ash Wednesday (S 55).

A calypso rhythm is apparent from the opening section of the poem in which a sense of movement, energy and increasing pace is created through the use of particular kinds of repetition such as anaphora. This is mirrored by the larger structural patterning of the poem: the repetition of the stanza beginning 'Symbol of the emancipated woman I come' and 'This mas I put on is not to hide me' at the opening and close of the poem (S 52, 74), the incrementally shifting focus on different aspects of carnival through the organizing motif of first hands, then feet, and finally streets, and the refrain-like unifying function of the meditative stanza which commences 'And is dih whole island/ Awash in a deep seasound . . .' (S 54, 68). Nichols has spoken of her protagonist being 'swept along by the all-embracing pulse of carnival . . . against the more constricting two-line rhyming beat' and her calypsonian-like 'resort to verbal self-inflation to make her voice heard' (S 5). Sections of the poem such as that beginning 'pour rum/ Beat gong . . .' (S 63) mimetically recreate the sounds and rhythms of carnival whilst others, such as the long section commencing with the question: "How hammer blows/ Can make such sweet tones . . .' engage not only with the sound and rhythm but also the aesthetic of steel pan, its ability to heal, to unify and to offer 'benediction' (S 68–70).

The incantatory, psalm-like section that follows is reminiscent of the tone and content of Jamaican George Campbell's poem, 'Holy'. Dating from the 1940s, a period of literary and cultural nationalism in Jamaica, 'Holy' can be read as an 'acknowledgement and benediction of the ethnic plurality on which a Caribbean nation could be built' (D&LW 117).[8] This section from 'sunris' is also reminiscent of Walcott's poetry in its valuing of the local, the people, their language and culture, and its ultimate recognition of, and reverence for, the spirituality of the everyday:

> Blessed is the first cool shadow of darkness
> Blessed is the deep well of our language
> Blessed is the space that the spirit inhabit
> Blessed is the robe we reserve for it
> Blessed is the need of our communion
> Blessed is the fire of our consecration

(S 71)

This mingling of the sacred and the profane in carnival, or in Nichols's words, the tension between 'pilgrimage' and 'the hedonist pull of carnival [as] spree' (S 5), is openly acknowledged by the protagonist when she describes carnival as 'blood beating/ And spirit moving free/ Is promiscuous wine/ Is sanctity' (S 54, 68). Appropriately enough, given the pre-Lenten timing of Trinidad carnival and the significant Catholic population of the island, the protagonist figures carnival as a secular version of the Mass, as echoed in the word 'mas' itself, and it is possible to see the multiple metamorphoses of carnival as secular echoes of transubstantiation: the mysterious transformation of bread and wine into the body and blood of Christ, which lies at the heart of the Catholic Mass.

Importantly however, in Nichols's poem as in real life, carnival is a thoroughly creolized and hybridized form, a symbol of cultural and ethnic hybridity in the Caribbean. Trinidadian novelist Earl Lovelace has Aldrick, a character in his novel *The Dragon Can't Dance*, say 'Real Carnival was a city thing, a Creole thing'.[9] As the protagonist of 'sunris' declares:

I'm a hybrid-dreamer
An ancestral-believer
A blood reveller
Who worship at the house of love

So Coolieman, Blackman, Redman[10] come,
Potageeman [Portuguese man], Chineyman, Whiteman, Brown,
Whoever throw they hand around mih waist
I come out to tasteup mih race

(S 52)

Indeed, part of the woman's self-discovery is that the deities of a range of different cultures, live – and are brought together – in the creolized ritual that is carnival. Thus the woman recognizes and addresses the Yoruba deities Legba, Ogun, Oya, Shango and Yemanja as well as Kali, Hindu goddess of destruction, the Amerindian Makonaima, the Christian Virgin Mary, the Greek goddess Iris and the Egyptian goddess Isis. Particularly effective is the woman's address to a personified Africa:

Africa? How to begin
after all this time and water?
I must begin by telling you

81

that your presence have endured
despite all the dark-despising
and death-dooming spread about you . . .

Africa, whenever I remember my father
soberly pouring a small libation in a corner
or my mother grinding fufu in her mortar
The simple burial of a navelstring –

I think of you too and I marvel
how your myriad rituals
have survived the crucible.
How they remain with us like relics
in the pillow of our unconscious . . .

(S 65–6)

The technique is very simple and yet startlingly effective; the woman is able to bridge both time and space in an ingenious way: rather than going to Africa, carnival brings Africa directly to her. Yet we are simultaneously reminded that this is 'playing mas' and that this is, in Brathwaite's words, 'Africa in the Caribbean'.[11] This is the significance of the woman's comment: 'Dih characters seem familiar/ but I can't quite remember it . . .' (S 73). An earlier comment by Nichols in interview illuminates this part of the poem: 'I keep being amazed at how much of Africa still remains in the Caribbean, when you consider the disruption caused by slavery and the whole European colonizing experience. You have the presence and influence of the indigenous peoples in the region too' (LN 96).

The indigenous Amerindians are introduced through the protagonist's encounter with Montezuma, 'Aztec . . . king . . . at the time of the arrival of the Spanish conquistadors in the early sixteenth century' (S 84). As Nichols explains in her notes to 'sunris':

Through a series of bizarre coincidence, Cortes, leader of the Spanish invaders was looked upon as the returning god, Quetzal-coatl, come back as legend had predicted, to claim his king-dom.Quetzalcoatl whose name meant 'feathered Serpent' was said to have come down from heaven . . . in the form of a priest-king. He ruled for a while but was driven out by the old tribal God, Tezcatlipoca. Quetzalcoatl was said to have . . . made the prophecy

'I will return in Ce Acatl (One Reed Year) and re-establish my rule. It will be a time of great tribulation for the people.' He then disappeared towards the East. The priests described him as having white skin and full beard and claimed that he would be wearing black on his return.

Amazingly Cortes landed in Mexico ... in the year 1519, a one Reed Year on the Aztec calendar. He was wearing black because it was Good Friday ... Montezuma, already agitated by a series of events which he saw as ill omens (including the appearance of a comet and the eruption of a volcano), sent forth glorious gifts to Cortes, thinking that perhaps this 'God' would be pacified and return to the east. But this only wetted the appetite of the conquistadors and what eventually ensued was the destruction of that whole civilization. (S 84–5)

Nichols has commented that:

ever since I did [Caribbean] history as a child ... Montezuma has ... always haunted my imagination ... So it is significant that the woman finds herself beside Montezuma in the whole sweep of carnival ... [of] all these characters that people taking part in carnival ... transform themselves [into, that] on that particular day ... she should find herself next to him. And this dialogue she has, well I think I was trying to place the Amerindian ... contribution ... into some focus [because] it's often ... neglected in literary discussions ... I wanted to ... have the woman engage in that kind of dialogue where she's questioning him about his role towards ... the Europeans ... the Spanish conquistadors who went out into the New World after Columbus's so-called discovery. (WH)

The Caribbean's 'first peoples' are also represented in 'sunris' by the figure of Makonaima, 'the Great Spirit of many Amerindian tribes' (S 84) and by 'Kanaima and the deathcrew', the Amerindian figure of death and vengeance and his henchmen.

More poignantly, Nichols alludes in the poem to the 'Sauteur leap ... of our indigenous ones' (S 69). This is a reference to the thousands of Amerindians, the Caribbean's original, indigenous peoples, who leapt from a cliff to their deaths in the sea rather than be captured by the conquering Europeans. Similarly, the carnival sound of the 'underbelly [steel] pan/ with dih innerbelly/ stars' recalls the other 'underbelly people', the millions of African slaves drowned in

83

'the old pirate water ... of the middle passage' (*S* 69). The invocation to 'scatter/ like minnows/ the shadows/ of Jonestown' refers to the Jonestown massacre of 1978 in which the Reverend Jim Jones's followers killed themselves by drinking poisoned Kool-Aid, a soft drink.[12] In this way absences are registered as presences and carnival is seen to symbolically heal the horrors of the past. As the woman reflects:

> I slipping past the old ship
> watching symbol of ship
> turn symbol of flowering tree
> as if imagination
> is the only hope for reality

(*S* 67)

The protagonist's self-naming at the end of the poem ('I just done christen myself, "sunris"', *S* 74) is important for a number of reasons, not least her inscription of herself, as a female subject, into the formerly male-dominated discourses of carnival. Nichols has spoken in interview of this self-naming as

> a kind of mythic coinage because ... it comes about through my own obsession or love of the sun [laughs] ... And it's also that 'ris' ending because my mother's name was Iris and Iris was supposed to be the goddess, the rainbow goddess in Greek mythology, a bridging type of figure ... my mother was very much that, she really reached across towards ... all kinds of racial strands, cultural and so on ... so that coining sunris was for me an important type of mythic ending ... Isis, the Egyptian goddess,[13] Iris, and so. (*WH*)[14]

The merging of the mother and mythic foremothers in the female protagonist's self-naming reflects Ostriker's point that 'Mothers, daughters, sisters must be recovered as parts "of the original woman we are"' (AO 218) as well as the 'recognition that the faces in mythology may be our faces which we "must explore" to gain knowledge of myth's inner meanings' (AO 214). As the protagonist wryly puts it:

> Columbus, you is not the only one
> Who can make discovery

(*S* 72)

5

'A Writer across Two Worlds'

> We do return and leave and return again, criss-crossing
> the Atlantic, but whichever side of the Atlantic we are on,
> the dream is always on the other side.
>
> — Pauline Melville, *Shape-Shifter*[1]

> Home is always elsewhere.
>
> — Fred D'Aguiar, 'Home'[2]

> You say you're civilised
> a kind of pride
> ask, 'Are you going back sometime?'
>
> but of course
> home is where the heart   lies
>
> — Grace Nichols, 'Fear' (*FBW* 28)

i is a long memoried woman, *Starting the Flying Fish* and 'sunris'
testify to the versatility of the trope of the journey, used by
Nichols to explore a continuum of cultures, temporal, psychic
and territorial spaces. However, the focus of this chapter is on
the twentieth-century journeying of both Nichols and her
poetic personae, as Caribbean migrants to Britain. In her own
words, Nichols 'migrated' to the UK with partner John Agard,
in 1977. Since then, she has returned to the Caribbean many
times but continues to live in Britain. In a recent interview
Kwame Dawes suggested: 'As a poet living in "exile" (and I
use that term guardedly), there must be an increasing tension
between the competing landscapes of your imagination', and
asked Nichols: 'How do you resolve this tension as a black
woman living in Britain . . .?' (KD 136). Nichols's response is
worth quoting in full:

the tension is very much there; I don't think it could be reconciled. You try to reconcile it. But the tension is always there and maybe it's a good thing ... it's not only the tension of physical difference between Guyana (or the Caribbean) and England, it's also in terms of language, culture – Creole versus Standard English, for example ... at a day-to-day level ... the tension is felt in very concrete ways ... I might be walking down the street ... and suddenly both landscapes collide – the English and the Caribbean; the gray becomes blue, the trees grow hibiscuses or whatever – in your mind's eye, just for some moments, there is a sense of unreality. A lot of my work still comes out of the Caribbean, in terms of what really excites me at a deep level, but more recently, I have been writing about England. And I've ... been getting into the English landscape, more especially in my latest collection, *Sunris*. (KD 136–7)

Dawes's notion of 'competing landscapes of the imagination' is a useful one in relation to Nichols's work and will be a focus of discussion in this chapter. The chapter also considers the complexities of 'home' in Nichols's work, as a migrant writer or 'writer across two worlds',[3] as well as the representation of Guyana in her writing. This includes discussion of her 1986 novel *Whole of a Morning Sky*.

The first epigraph to the chapter is taken from Guyanese-born, British-based Pauline Melville's short story 'Eat Labba and Drink Creek Water'. Melville's story derives its title from the popular belief amongst Guyanese that if they eat Labba, a native animal, and 'drink Creek Water' they are destined to return one day to their country.[4] Like *i is* and 'sunris', the fragmented form of 'Eat Labba' can be seen as 'paradigmatic of the larger fragmentations of Caribbean history'. At the heart of the story is a 'sequence of "journeys", arrivals and departures' (C&L 164). Melville, like Nichols, explores the 'trope of the journey in its various permutations ... imaginative and dream journeying, the journeys of the dead ... as well as literal migrations, quests and odysseys and a series of voyages into the archives of personal memory and a collective past. Like a number of texts by Caribbean writers based in Britain,[5] [Melville's story] is concerned with the problems of return to the Caribbean and specifically with the overlapping versions of Guyana which are encountered in myth, dream, and the different expectations and realities' (C&L 165). Barbadian novelist and critic George Lamming famously wrote of the West Indian's passage to Britain as a 'journey to an expectation'[6] and this 'journey to an expectation' is inverted in the opening pages of Melville's story as the narrator and her Jamaican friend discuss their mutual need to 'go back'. However, the story goes on to deconstruct this easy duality by acknowledging the complex trajectories of desire which accompany such journeys and which problematize any concept of 'home', 'return' or 'arrival' (C&L 165). This is just one of the ways in which 'Boundaries are continually crossed and blurred ... in this, the most impressionistic and autobiographical of Melville's stories, [as] the narrator weaves an anancy-like fictional web which bridges time and space, past and present, the real and the mythical, the natural and supernatural, London and the Caribbean' (C&L 165–6).

Fred d'Aguiar is, like Nichols, a black British/Guyanese writer whose punningly titled collection *British Subjects* (1993) focuses on the realities of black life in Britain. The poem 'Home', from which the epigraph is taken, focuses much more directly on the ambivalences attendant on this traversing of continents and cultures and on the complexities of being black and a British citizen. D'Aguiar's recognition that 'home is always elsewhere', at once removed, displaced, deferred is a common enough trope in postcolonial literatures, especially in relation to those who continually cross boundaries, whether territorial boundaries or the 'dominantly construed and ever shifting boundaries of race, gender and class'.[7] But the twist in this particular poem is that the poetic persona is referring to Britain, rather than the Caribbean, as 'Home':

> These days whenever I stay away too long,
> anything I happen to clap eyes on,
> (that red telephone box) somehow makes me
> miss here more than anything I can name.
>
> My heart performs a jazzy drum-beat
> When the crow's feet on the 747
> Scrape down at Heathrow ...
>
> ... Grey light and close skies I love you.
> chokey streets, roundabouts and streetlamps
> with tyres chucked round them, I love you.[8]

87

Yet, in this and other poems in the collection, D'Aguiar communicates the fact that Britain is, for him, simultaneously home and a place of manifold exclusions and racist realities, as it is for many other black Britons. In short, Britain is home and not home, a place of belonging and unbelonging. This is also a recurrent concern in Nichols's work, notably the poems of the 'In Spite of Ourselves' section of *Lazy Thoughts of a Lazy Woman* (pp. 27–36).

The migrant's complex sense of 'doubleness', of belonging to more than one place and more than one culture, is thrown into stark relief by the explicitly monocultural assumptions voiced by a representative of the host society in 'Fear' (*FBW* 28), from which the third epigraph is taken. Like a number of poems by other black British women writers,[9] Nichols's poem raises important issues of national, ethnic and cultural identity. She contrasts the ideal of a harmoniously multicultural Britain, reductively figured as 'black music enrich/ food spice up', with the reality of

> Our culture rub[bing] skin
> Against your own
> Bruising awkward as plums

The poem plays upon different meanings of 'Fear': the slippage between the host society's fear of the 'other' and the poetic persona's more informed fear and concern for black British youth and for her own child:

> Sometimes I grow afraid
> Too many young blacks
> Reaping seconds
> Indignant cities full of jail
>
> I think my child's too loving
> For this fear

Similarly, Nichols emphasizes a dual meaning to the word 'lies' within the familiar phrase 'home is where the heart lies', by isolating it on a single line. Accordingly, home signifies doubly: it is where one is happy but may also be a place which the heart 'lies' about, a version of home misrepresented through memory or nostalgia. This is particularly relevant if home is taken by the migrant writer to be the Caribbean.

However, any idealization of the Caribbean in Nichols's poem is quashed by the persona's recognition of the harsh realities of the region's politics. As Nichols subtly infers, there is also cause for 'fear' back home':

> I come from a backyard
> Where the sun reaches down ...
> Mangoes fall to the ground
> Politicians turn cruel clowns

In this way the poem resists easy oppositionalities between Britain and 'back home'.

'Island Man' (*FBW* 29) is one of a number of poems which connect Britain with the Caribbean. Nichols has spoken of the poem being inspired by her experiences when she first moved to Britain:

> I lived in Neasden which is quite near the North Circular Road and ... 'Island Man' came because I myself woke up and the kind of 'swoosh' of the traffic, the big industrial lorries going by ... reminded me of the sound of the sea back home. So the idea for the poem came from that, of having this Island man wake up and think he's back in the Caribbean. In actual fact he's very much in London. (*PGN*)

As Nichols suggests, the poem is unified by its overlapping imagery: 'the sound of blue surf ... breaking and wombing' and the 'surge of wheels/ ... dull North Circular roar'. However, the gradual alignment of internal and external landscapes is also achieved through the use of near homophones or near puns ('sand' for 'sounds') and the dual meaning of 'heaves' (to hoist oneself upward but also to vomit, be seasick), in the final part of the poem.

The prevailing greyness of Britain in 'Island Man', the 'grey metallic roar' as contrasted to the 'blue surf' of the Island man's 'small emerald isle', link it to another poem from this collection set in London, 'Two Old Black Men on a Leicester Square Park Bench' (*FBW* 35). In 'Two Old Black Men' the poem's persona wonders about the possible interior landscapes of her subjects, the discrepancy between their migrant present and their Caribbean past:

> Do you dream of revolutions
> You could have forged
> Or mourn
> Some sunfull woman you
> Might have known a
> Hibiscus flower
> Ghost memories of desire

For these old men, as for others in Nichols's poetry, the past really is a foreign country; it is the Caribbean.[10] Moreover, the poem reveals how ' "Home" is a mythic place of desire in the diasporic imagination. In this sense it is a place of no-return, even if it is possible to visit the geographical territory that is seen as the place of "origin" ' (AB 192). As in 'Fear', the observing persona suggests that such nostalgic, idealized constructions of 'back home' have always coexisted uneasily with a very different Caribbean reality, now diluted by distance and time:

> ... it's easy
> to rainbow the past
> after all the letters from
> home spoke of hardships
>
> and the sun was traded long ago

Significantly, Nichols's use of creole is less marked in poems of regret and resignation such as this, than in bolder, more optimistic poems of migration such as 'Beverley's Saga' (LTLW 35–7).

The final lines of 'Two Old Black Men ...' are echoed in a more recent poem by Nichols, 'First Generation Monologue' (S 31–3). This opens with the lines: 'Like every other Caribbean émigré/ who'd put away the lamp of the sun/ She spoke of the bad old migrant days:/ I was in the ship's first wave' (S 31). As in a number of other poems in Sunris ('Red', 'Black', 'White' (S 9–11)) there is an acute sensitivity to colour in the poem. The speaker contrasts the vital abundance of colour in the Caribbean (the red of hibiscus, the green of ivy, the 'memories blue as the indigo/ of my mother's rinsing water' which sustain her by 'light[ing] my days', S 31) with the sterile, sluggish, lack of colour in Britain. As the persona admits:

> ... I never realise it would have been
> so cold and grey, so damp and dull ...
>
> Eternity was greyness to me, I tell you,
> The days I dragged myself across the days,
> Barely managing, snail-like
> Under that amorphous octopus of a sky.
> The days I got my colours mixed –
> a dream of colours –
> on my brain's muddled palette
>
> (*S* 31–2)

The poem reflects what Nichols has termed the 'sense of unreality' (KD 136–7) experienced by the migrant in Britain, but this unreal state also facilitates some startling new insights, glimpses into a Britain both familiar and strange. As John McLeod argues, with reference to 'Imaginary Homelands', a key critical essay by another migrant writer, Salman Rushdie:

> The migrant seems in a better position than others to realise that all systems of knowledge, all views of the world, are never totalising, whole or pure, but incomplete, muddled and hybrid. To live as a migrant may well evoke the pain of loss and of not being firmly rooted in a secure place; but it is also to live in a world of immense possibility with the realisation that new knowledges and ways of seeing can be constructed ... In these terms, the space of the 'in-between' becomes rethought as a place of immense creativity and possibility ... (JM 215)

Arguably, Nichols's portrayal of the migrant's experience of post-war Britain in this poem is as gritty as that which is to be found in parts of the novels of George Lamming, Sam Selvon or Andrew Salkey dating from the period (the 1950s and 1960s).[11] However, 'First Generation Monologue' is markedly untouched by the kind of humour found in Selvon's fiction. Asked in interview if some of the poems in *Sunris* 'capture a disappointment with this country', Nichols replied:

> Well, no not really a disappointment ... it's just [that] some of the poems [are] based on memory ... you know talking with older women ... and I'm trying to be truthful to that experience, for example, the first generation monologue of the first generation immigrant woman who came here in the fifties, her experiences ...

things were very hard . . . [in] Britain just after the war and . . . they were the first set of immigrants. (*WH*)

Heidi Mirza has argued that recuperating the oral histories, testimonies, and life stories of such women is absolutely crucial. This is because

> official statistics and texts written about and documenting the main period of postcolonial migration from the 1940s to the 1960s writes out the female story of postcolonial migration. What remains is for us to gather the snippets of black women's stories as they emerge to challenge their negation and disrupt the neat telling of those times.[12]

Nichols's poem can thus be seen to contribute, in its own way, to this larger project: the need for black British women to reclaim agency and self-determination through the 'telling of who we are'.[13]

'Wherever I Hang' (*LTLW* 10) treats similar subject matter but in a very different way. As a creole monologue or voice-portrait, it belongs to a particularly rich tradition within Caribbean poetry, as pioneered by early figures such as Claude McKay, Una Marson and Louise Bennett, and adapted by poets as varied as Valerie Bloom, James Berry, David Dabydeen and John Agard.[14] The poem's persona recalls how 'I leave me people, me land, me home/ For reasons, I not too sure'. She charts her progress from the dream-like unreality of first contact with England, through to gradual acculturation:

> And so, little by little
> I begin to change my calypso ways
> Never visiting nobody
> Before giving them clear warning
> And waiting me turn in queue

As she admits:

> I get accustom to de English life
> But I still miss back-home side
> To tell you de truth
> I don't know really where I belaang

The use of a creole idiom is important in this and other poems. As Carole Boyce Davies suggests: 'The deliberate fracturing of the English word disrupts from outside the contained identity of Englishness as expressed in its language'.[15] The poem ends, boldly and unexpectedly with the brilliantly simple compromise:

> Yes, divided to de ocean
> Divided to de bone
>
> Wherever I hang my knickers – that's my home.

'Beverley's Saga' (*LTLW* 35–7) deals with the experiences of a younger generation who identify themselves as 'Black British'. Nichols uses the ballad form, most extensively used by earlier Caribbean poets such as Claude McKay and Louise Bennett, but also an integral part of the prose style of Sam Selvon in his early London-based novels and short stories.[16] Indeed, the line 'Summer is hearts' which appears in the third and final stanzas of 'Beverley's Saga' and which is also the title of a children's poem by Nichols[17] is taken from the remarkable, lyrical section of Selvon's classic novel of West Indian life in London, *The Lonely Londoners*, in which Moses, the central character, celebrates summer in the city in his own inimitable style.

The poem's subject came to England from her birthplace, Jamaica, at the age of 3 and recalls how her father fought for the Mother Country, as did a significant number of West Indians, in the Second World War. The poem is partly a challenge issued to the ordinary woman in the street, as well as those in positions of power or authority, such as the politician and the policeman, to recognize that Beverley is *British* ('Dis ya she country', *LTLW* 35). It is also an exercise in consciousness-raising, as to the centuries-old black presence in Britain and the important role of West Indians' African slave ancestors, whose labour on the sugar plantations produced the wealth that is reflected in some of Britain's finest eighteenth- and early nineteenth-century buildings. In response to the 'ole English lady' who stops her to ask if she is on holiday in Britain, Beverley issues a lesson in black but also crucially, *British* history:

> . . . leh me tell you lickle history –
> You see all did big fat architectry?
> In it is de blood of my ancestry.
> Dis black presence go back
> Two, three century . . .
>
> (*LTLW* 36)

Alluding to the observation most famously made by Louise Bennett in her poem 'Colonisation in Reverse', Beverley continues:

> ... In any case, you been my country first,
> So we come back inna kinda reverse.

(*LTLW* 37)

However, unlike the blunt address to policeman and politician, Beverley's tone towards the old lady is never hostile. Indeed, the poem ends with the warmth of Beverley's invitation to come back to her flat for that most English of refreshments, 'a lickle cup-o-tea'.

In other poems, the centrality of migration to the history of the Caribbean is picked up in subtler ways. Readings of 'The Fat Black Woman Goes Shopping' (*FBW* 11) usually concentrate on the poem's satirical assault on Western notions of beauty and 'appropriate' female behaviour. However, the poem's meanings resonate far beyond this immediate context. As so often in Nichols's poetry, this depth depends on the slippage of meaning in a single word or phrase. Thus the use of the apparently straightforward adjective 'accommodating' signifies much more than the need for the fat black woman to finding clothes large enough to fit her ample form. It also signals a wider concern with the ambivalent experience of life in Britain for the fat black woman, that sense of belonging here but also elsewhere, which is also the subject of other poems in the collection. This 'elsewhere' is simultaneously the 'back-home' of the Caribbean, but also that other 'Mother Country', beyond it: Africa. Similarly, when the fat black woman 'curses in Swahili/ Yoruba/ and nation language under her breathing/ *all this journeying and journeying*' (my emphasis), not only is her alter/native language choice important in signifying defiance, but the line 'all this journeying and journeying' also refers to a much longer history of migrations of her people, not just the immediate context of her journeying from London 'store to store'.

In 'We New World Blacks' (*FBW* 30), the Caribbean provides more comforting cultural sustenance to the diasporic black. The poem recognizes certain continuities with the Caribbean. 'However far/ we've been' (*FBW* 30). Chief amongst these is language, the distinctive 'timbre' which persists as a rooted reminder of origins:

> The timbre
> in our voice
> betrays us
> however far
> we've been
>
> whatever tongue
> we speak
> the old ghost
> asserts itself
> in dusky echoes
>
> like driftwood traces

Appropriately enough, given the sea-journeys of the Middle Passage and the mid-twentieth-century migration of West Indians to Britain, Nichols chooses the image of 'driftwood traces', melded and softened by the sea, to describe the 'echoes' in the voices of these 'New World blacks'. However, the major allusion in this quietly unassuming but beautifully resonant poem, is to the African-Caribbean practice of burying a child's 'navel string' (umbilical cord) under a tree in a yard or garden near to their place of birth:[18]

> In spite of
> ourselves
> we know the way
> back to
>
> the river stone
>
> the little decayed
> spirit
> of the navel string
> hiding in our back garden.

The 'navel string' is not only a culturally specific reminder of origins but also functions in this poem as a metonym for birth, beginnings, family and 'back home' more generally. In this way the poem is made to carry tremendous emotional freight with economy and grace.

A variation on this nostalgic look back to Caribbean origins is 'Like a Beacon' (*FBW* 27), in which the poem's persona admits:

95

> In London
> Every now and then
> I get this craving
> For my mother's food
> I leave art galleries
> In search of plantains
> Saltfish
> sweet potatoes.

Like the African-American concept of 'soul-food', Caribbean food functions in this poem as a 'link . . . this touch of home . . . a beacon against the cold'. 'Praisesong for My Mother' and 'Why Shouldn't She?' (*FBW* 44) also use these images of cooking and of food as nurture to signify links between the mother and motherland and to signal the cultural specificity of 'home'.

'Out of Africa' (*LTLW* 30) is often overlooked as a relatively 'light-weight' poem. However, despite its jaunty tone, it deserves attention, not least because of its ingenious mingling of truths and cultural stereotypes. In this way, we are reminded that Africa, the Caribbean and Britain, are, in the migrant's consciousness, essentially constructed through and by the ways they are represented in dominant discourses.

Nichols's admission in a recent interview that 'I've . . . been getting into the English landscape, more especially in my latest collection, *Sunris*' (KD 137) is borne out in several poems in this collection, including 'Long-Man' (*S* 13–15) and 'Hurricane' (*S* 34–5). Although Nichols writes of the natural environment in a British context in poems such as 'Spring' (*FBW* 34), 'Winter-Widow' (*LTLW* 15) and 'Conkers' (*LTLW* 47), she does so in quite abstract terms. It is very rare for her to engage with the rural landscapes of Britain in any particularized or specific way. In 'Long-Man' she does exactly this, taking as her starting point, a visit with friends and family to one of England's most ancient chalk hill carvings: the Long-Man of Wilmington on the South Downs. As Nichols describes in her notes to *Sunris*:

> The Long-Man, or Green Man . . . continues to mystify generations of visitors and there is still much speculation whether . . . he is Saxon, Celtic or even Roman in origin . . . naked, featureless and enigmatic. The silent figure of the Long-Man with his two staves invites us to solve the mystery. (*S* 84)

As in 'sunris' this trip is referred to as a mythic-spiritual journey: 'this our hill-god pilgrimage' (*S* 13), but it is an altogether more tongue-in-cheek reference given the more grounded journey undertaken here. Indeed, the journeyers are literally in danger of being grounded, impeded by the 'caking-blood/ Of England's sod', despite 'the timeless witchery/ Of the landscape' (*S* 13, 14). As in D'Aguiar's poem 'Home', where even the customs officers speak 'with surrey loam caked/ on the tongue', Nichols's use of the word 'sod' functions both literally and metonymically. It invokes a particularly potent myth of England, that of Shakespeare's green and 'sceptered isle . . . other Eden, demi paradise . . . [t]his blessed plot, this earth, this realm, this England',[19] only to undermine it with literalized images of 'caking' and 'sod'. Yet the residual suggestion remains in the phrase 'caking blood' that the English landscape is a historical text, a palimpsest of historical and cultural associations which can be 'read' or interpreted in particular ways. These may even act to exclude the migrant or post-colonial subject, as Trinidadian writer, V. S. Naipaul suggests in his 1987 novel, *The Enigma of Arrival*.

Nichols's 'Long-Man' also involves revisionist mythmaking of a kind, as the poem's main persona refers to herself as 'a wiser Demeter' and to 'the Presumptuous Goddess in me' (*S* 13, 15). The party of walkers wonder about the meaning of the Long-Man, their language and interpretations casting him variously as a Christian figure: ('nailing him with a/ Crucifixion of questions' and 'Poor wounded man/ . . . staves in his arms', *S* 14, 15); a pagan fertility symbol or 'presage of a new androgyny' (*S* 14); a figure of death ('The gatekeeper-reaper/ Who would reap us all in', *S* 15); and then, significantly, in terms of Caribbean folklore: like the figure of 'Moongazer',[20] as trickster-like, a 'cunning chameleon . . . tricking our eyeballs' (*S* 15). The implication of the latter description is that the Long-Man is himself a shape-shifter; it is not just a matter of multiple interpretations being applied to him – he is *all* these things.

The poem ends with 'The presumptuous/ goddess in me' (*S* 15) reading the Long-Man as a figure unable to guard himself against the power of female desire:

> The staves in his arms
> No barrier to a woman like
> She-who-would-break-them
> And take him in her arms

(S 15)

In the 1980s a number of black British artists, such as photographer Ingrid Pollard, worked on projects which sought to explore and address the invisibility of black people in English rural landscapes. Pollard argued that, for the black subject, locating oneself in relation to the English countryside was problematic for several reasons. Historically, the black presence in Britain has been associated with urban rather than rural landscapes (a demographic factor which still prevails). Moreover, many of the versions of the English countryside presented in paintings and literary texts are so revered, so familiar and so potent that they have tended to drown out alternative representations and ways of seeing the same landscapes. Furthermore, such dominant representations can act to marginalize or exclude the black presence by subscribing to a version of 'Englishness predicated on an essentialized and mythical monoculturalism. All these factors make it difficult for black subjects to locate themlves within, and feel 'at home' in, British rural landapes. Nichols's 'Long-Man' can be seen in part as an interesting intervention in these debates. Indeed, her poem seems to counter Pollard's observations, revealing, for her at least, a new accommodation, or 'at-homeness' in the landscape.

A very different poem which also involves reading the landscape is 'Hurricane Hits England' (S 34–5). In this poem the poetic persona admits: 'It took a hurricane, to bring her closer/ To the landscape' (S 34). The unleashing of such powerful elemental forces seems to her 'Like some dark ancestral spectre' both 'Fearful and reassuring' (S 34). Accordingly, she invokes the Yoruba gods Oya and Shango, gods of the wind and thunder and lightning respectively.[21] She also invokes Huracan, the South American god of the winds, from which the English word 'hurricane' is derived. She asks for meaning:

> What is the meaning of old tongues
> Reaping havoc
> In new places? . . .
>
> What is the meaning of trees
> Falling heavy as whales
> Their crouched roots
> Their cratered graves?
>
> O why is my heart unchained?

(S 34–5)

The imagery of the poem, deliberately echoes a distant slave past ('The howling ship of the wind', 'dark ancestral spectre', 'cratered graves', 'heart unchained', S 34–5) but also stresses African continuities, Africa persisting in its deities. The gods are not lost or dead, but alive[22] and present in this most unlikely of places the 'English coast' (S 34). Accordingly she declares:

> Tropical Oya of the Weather,
> I am aligning myself to you,
> I am following the movements of your winds,
> I am riding the mystery of your storm.

(S 35)

They represent not the past but the present and, by implication, the future. The epiphany of the poem is thus that they are to be found even in this diasporic location, for 'the earth is the earth is the earth' (S 35).

'BACK HOME CONTEMPLATION'

In his book *Beginning Postcolonialism*, John McLeod argues that the migrant state involves replacing the 'grounded certainties of *roots* . . . with the transnational contingencies of *routes*' (JM 215) This study has focused on the diverse 'routes' historical, cultural, imaginative as well as physical, taken by Africans, West Indians and other peoples in their varied journeys, pilgrimages, sprees and migrations (both forced and voluntary). The final focus is on those journeys back to the Caribbean which are also frequently a return to childhood memories.

99

In a 1997 programme for British schools, Nichols took a journey back to Guyana and spoke of what it felt like to return. In his essay 'Imaginary Homelands', Salman Rushdie observes that for the migrant writer who has been 'away' for a long period, 'home' and 'homelands' become increasingly imaginary constructs, located not in an actual place but in the imagination. Rushdie argues:

> It may be that writers in my position, exiles or emigrants or expatriates, are haunted by some sense of loss, some urge to reclaim, to look back, even at the risk of being mutated into pillars of salt. But if we do look back, we must also do so in the knowledge – which gives rise to profound uncertainties – that our physical alienation from [our homelands] almost inevitably means that we will not be capable of reclaiming precisely the thing that was lost; that we will, in short, create fictions, not actual cities or villages, but invisible ones, imaginary homelands.[23]

As an always partially remembered place, 'home' is subject to all the fragility, fragmentation and unreliability inherent in memory; as the focus of intense longing and desire, it becomes an even more complex location. Interestingly, Nichols's remarks at the outset of her journey reflect some of Rushdie's insights:

> it's difficult at times going back to your past because you know that past has really changed and you've changed too; so you can never go back to a place and find it exactly as you left it; so there's a lot of emotional turmoil ... When you're making a trip it brings things into focus that you haven't finished, at the same time you're looking forward ... to reconnecting with the landscape ... so it's a big journey. (PGN)

Such a reconnection is the subject of 'Timehri Airport to Georgetown' (S 43). Nichols has spoken of the Guyanese landscape as very important to her writing. Unlike many Caribbean countries, Guyana is not an island but is part of the South American mainland. It has an 'exterior', the flat coastal plains where the Dutch colonists originally settled from the late sixteenth century onwards, and later, in the eighteenth and early nineteenth century, the English. Most of the population still live on this narrow coastal plain. It also has an 'interior', a vast expanse of Amazonian rainforest which covers some 85 per cent of the country and, in the south, are grass-covered savannahs. It is in the interior that the majority of the indigenous Amerindian people live. Guyana is about the size of the US state of Idaho and yet it only has a population of about 700,000. This duality, and the extraordinary nature of this 'hinterland' has compelled and inspired many Guyanese writers. These include Pauline Melville, and most notably Wilson Harris who worked as a surveyor in the interior before becoming a writer. Nichols has said of the interior:

> no one who experiences the Guyana hinterland remains unchanged – the magnitude and density of the forests, the sudden sheer drop, when flying by helicopter, over a mountain's stark face, the dark mysterious rivers and waterfalls, all leave their primeval imprint on the psyche forever.
>
> It wasn't surprising that the very first adult short story I ever wrote was set in this region. I also began research into collecting Guyanese folktales and Amerindian myths, some of which appear in a small self-published collection for children, *Baby Fish and other Stories*. (HT 297)

In 'For Forest' (*LTLW* 45), Nichols personifies Forest as a woman who 'could keep secrets', one who listens but 'don't broadcast her business'. Her dreams map the beginnings of time and a mythical as well as historical Guyanese past:

> Forest dreaming about mountain
> and when the earth was young
> Forest dreaming of the caress of gold
> Forest rootsing with mysterious eldorado

And at night, she becomes a fearful supernatural entity, 'a bad dream woman'. Nichols has spoken of the poem coming to her:

> while lying under my quilt one . . . winter . . . morning in London . . . the whole mystery and magic of the Guyana rainforests came back to me, the sounds of the waterfalls, birdsounds, the sounds of the insects. And forest, for me, became like a woman letting her hair down to all this music. (*PGN*)

The final line of 'For Forest' is inflected with social and ecological commitment: 'And we must keep Forest', a characteristic also found in other of Nichols's poems set in the Caribbean.

POEMS OF SOCIAL COMMENT

Poems which engage with the complex issues raised by the status of many Caribbean islands as tourist destinations abound in Caribbean literature.[24] Tourism is not a major industry in Guyana, for it is not 'like the rest of the Caribbean in terms of blue seas and white beaches; it's very much South American in terms of the landscape' (*PGN*). Despite this, Nichols has published a number of poems which deal with the topic. These include 'Price We Pay for the Sun' (*FBW* 42) and 'On Receiving a Jamaican Postcard' (*LTLW* 23).

The project of 'Price We Pay' is to defamiliarize the image of the 'islands [as] picture postcards' and to remind the reader of the realities behind the image. Thus the poem's persona urges:

> These islands real
> More real
> Than flesh and blood
> Past stone
> Past foam
> These islands split
> Bone

Such visceral images remind the reader of the monumental human cost behind what the tourist sees on the surface, in the contemporary Caribbean, primarily, of course, the historical fact of slavery. However, the poem also intimates that the legacies of this history, both psychological and economic, have been equally devastating. In Nichols's poem, 'Poverty is the price/ we pay for the sun'.

In 'On Receiving a Jamaican Postcard' (*LTLW* 23), Nichols returns to this picture-postcard mentality, the tourist-eye view of the Caribbean. That this poem is written in nation language is perhaps not incidental, for the creole idiom cuts through the staged absurdity of the dancers on the postcard:

> He staging a dance-prance
> Head in a red band
> Beating he waist drum
> As if he want to drown she wid sound
> An yes, he muscle looking strong

> She vision of frilly red
> Back-backing too he riddim
> Exposing she brown leg
> Arcing like lil mo
> She will limbo into de sea.

Nichols is clearly satirizing the spurious construction of 'cultural authenticity' within the scene, and the postcard's tired rehearsal of racial stereotypes ('he muscle looking strong', 'she will limbo into de sea'. However, what is interesting about the poem is the ambiguity of the figures of the dancers. Are they complicit in the staging of this tourist-eye version of the Caribbean? Or is there the possibility of a carefully concealed mimicry in the description of 'de two a dem in smiling conspiracy'. In the ambivalent space between the two possibilities, an immensely subversive agency is unleashed. The postcolonial theorist Homi Bhabha terms this 'colonial mimicry', mimicry combining the dual sense of slavish imitation and subversive mimicry of the way in which they are discursively constructed (in this case by the tourist postcard), the activity they are engaged in, the role they are asked to play.[25]

Other poems engage with the social, economic and political realities of the Caribbean and reflect on the changes which have occurred in Guyana since Nichols left in 1977. They include 'Walking With My Brother in Georgetown' (*LTLW* 39) and 'Blackout' (*S* 44). In 'Walking With My Brother in Georgetown', a female persona, who may well be Nichols herself, returns to the city where she once lived and finds it much changed:

> Dih trenches seem smaller
> Dih streets
> Dih houses
> An everyting an everybody
> Look suh rundown
> An stamp wih dih dry an hunger

She calls it a 'dying' city, reflects that 'We need a purging/ New fires burning'. The apocalyptic imagery of destruction and cleansing in these lines echoes other Caribbean poems such as Derek Walcott's *Epitaph for the Young* (1949)[26] or Martin

103

Carter's 'Good Friday, 1962', as well as parts of *Whole of a Morning Sky*. Significantly, the poem is dated August 1984, and in it the Jonestown massacre of 1978 and the assassination of Dr Walter Rodney, leader of the multiracial independent Marxist party (WPA), in 1980 in Guyana, are described as amongst the 'too many deaths unmourning' (*S* 40). Return, for the poem's persona at least, is a dispiriting journey into disillusionment.

A later poem from *Sunris* returns to this theme. The immediate context of 'Blackout' (*S* 44) is the strange and shadowy world of a city during a powercut, but its larger theme is the chaos of everyday life in a severely economically strained contemporary Guyana.[27] The poem opens with startling images of the Guyanese's bat-like adaptation to the frequent blackouts:

> People have grown sixthsense
> And sonic ways, like bats,
> Emerging out of the shadows
> into the light of their own flesh

As the poem's persona reflects, it seems as if 'we're in some thirdworld movie'. This sense of unreality is also created by the recurrent cinematic imagery, and use of striking perspective in the poem:

> ... everywhere there are flittings
> and things coming into being
> in a night where football is a game of faith

Despite its subject matter, the tone of the poem is lyrical and almost elegiac. The real indictments of this poem, however, come in glimpses of

> ... children ... hovering,
> hopeful moths around the flickerless Box
> immune to the cloying stench of toilets
> that can't be flushed. The children
> all waiting on electric spell to come
> and trigger a movie, the one featuring America,
> played out endlessly in their heads.

Television and cinema are the new vehicles of colonialism of a cultural and economic kind, also termed neo-colonialism or cultural imperialism in what Trinidad writer Merle Hodge has termed a 'more vicious era of cultural penetration' (SC 205). Such a presence in Guyana as in other postcolonial territories effectively militates against true sovereignty or the development of 'an "independent" post-colonial Caribbean culture' as the editors of *The Routledge Reader in Caribbean Literature* point out (D&LW 451).

As the poem suggests, this particular narrative is always the same, this state of affairs in Guyana depressingly like a 'worn-out movie, slow reeling/ Under the endless cinema of the skies' (*S* 45).

'CHILD-KINGDOM': POEMS OF CHILDHOOD

Unsurprisingly a significant number of Nichols's poems set in the Caribbean share Caribbean literature's recurrent concern with childhood. The biblical imagery of 'Childhood' (*FBW* 40) suggests childhood as an edenic place of freedom, a not uncommon rendering in Caribbean women's writing (see for example, Merle Hodge's *Crick Crack Monkey* (1970) and Jamaica Kincaid's *Annie John* (1985), but also, as for Gem, the young protagonist in *Whole of a Morning Sky*, a place of 'strange recurring mysteries' for the child (*FBW* 40). Elsewhere, Nichols conceives of childhood as a 'Child-Kingdom', a term which neatly conflates the temporal, spatial, imaginative and spiritual dimensions of childhood. In this poem, the language is similarly biblical in cadence:

> Now I return to my child-kingdom
> To my brownwater house of many mansions
> To my green and sunbaked pasturelands . . .
>
> (*LTLW* 42)

Indeed, the poem's persona imagines herself as godlike, a 'God-child' commanding the 'brown waters' and, like the Christ-child, worshipped by ordinary animals:

> cows sang for me
> Donkeys heralded me
> Sheep parted at my coming
>
> (*LTLW* 42)

In the programme, Nichols returned to the village where she spent the first eight years of her childhood. She described 'coming back to this place . . . [as] like coming face-to-face with my past and the spirit of my childhood' and admitted 'Memories of my childhood play a big part in my creative work as a whole' (*PGN*). Yet for her as for other 'writers across two worlds', return 'home' is always ambivalent: 'In one way it's like coming back . . . but at another level, you can never go back. It's very moving at that level: where you come from, your roots, your sense of place. It gives you that kind of special feeling but it doesn't mean you want to come back' (*PGN*).

A number of such poems of childhood have been collected in anthologies of her writing both for adults and for children. One such poem is 'Be a Butterfly' (*FBW* 49). Nichols has spoken of the preacher at the tiny village church she attended as a child, as the inspiration for this poem:

> I think I have a sense of humour and it comes out in my work. There was this preacher and we were all attending a Sunday Service, and he was using the metaphor of the butterfly to speak of . . . the higher life in a religious way. And he was really getting into it, and sweating it out, and almost screaming and shouting: 'Don't be a kyatahpilla!' he said, 'Be a butterfly!' And that has really stayed with me. We remember it from time to time as joke because we were laughing when he was serious. (*PGN*)

The use of creole is crucial in poems such as this, in which the speaking voice is absolutely central. Nichols has spoken of creole not only as the language of home, but also as a key constituent of her Caribbean identity:

> It's always refreshing, at another level, to hear the rhythms and sounds, that language. That's where you sprang from. You can't forget that; in a way that's what gave you life and your own unique identity. (*PGN*)

WHOLE OF A MORNING SKY

In Caribbean fiction as well as poetry, examples of the use of the trope of childhood and the bildungsroman form abound. Some critics argue that this outpouring of novels of childhood and semi-autobiographical writing is a logical component of literary nationalism and the emergence of a West Indian literary canon in the years surrounding independence in the Caribbean. Others, notably Fredric Jameson, have argued that such texts function in more specific ways as national allegories, reflecting the growth and development not just of their individual protagonists but also of their national collectivities.

A range of literary examples ranging from the 1950s to the 1980s might include Trinidadian Sam Selvon's *A Brighter Sun* (1952), Barbadian George Lamming's *In the Castle of My Skin* (1953), Trinidadian Michael Anthony's *The Year in San Fernando* (1965) and *Green Days by the River* (1967), Trinidadian Ian McDonald's *The Humming Bird Tree* (1969), Trinidadian Merle Hodge's *Crick Crack Monkey* (1970), Belizean Zee Edgell's *Beka Lamb* (1982), Guyanese Janice Shinebourne's *The Last English Plantation* (1988), Antiguan Jamaica Kincaid's *Annie John* (1985) and Trinidadian Ismith Khan's *A Day in the Country* (1994). To argue, as Jameson does, that all Third World texts and cultural productions are allegorical in this way[28] is obviously controversial and not a viewpoint shared by this study. However, Jameson's critical paradigm may be an enabling one in relation to Caribbean texts of this kind, if used discriminately and reflexively (that is with awareness of the paradigm's weaknesses and blind-spots).

It is certainly possible to read Nichols's first and only novel, *Whole of a Morning Sky*, in this way. Evelyn O'Callaghan does precisely this when she suggests 'the child Gem['s] . . . development is linked to that of her young and struggling nation' (EO 82). However, O'Callaghan goes on to develop her own more original and sophisticated analysis of the novel. These ways of reading *Whole of a Morning Sky* will therefore also be considered in this section.

Jamaican-born feminist critic Patricia Duncker goes as far as to argue that:

> What is really original in Nichols' *Whole of a Morning Sky* is not the method, nor the style, nor the writer's implicit perspectives, but the material itself. And this is a factor which emerges again and again in writing by Asian and Afro-Caribbean Blackwomen. This story has – quite simply – never been told.[29]

However, it's equally important to recognize that not all black women's writing is autobiographical and not all autobiographical writing by black women writers is purely or simply so. Gina Wisker makes this point when she cites Barbara Burford's observations on this misapprehension in relation to the politics of publishing black women's writing:

> While there is much autobiography produced by Black women writers, Burford argues that this itself can be a limitation, that there is a staggering arrogance in the assumption that this is all Black women writers *can* produce: 'the racism implicit in the presumption that we are somehow not "sophisticated" enough for fiction or fantasy is staggering' (Burford, p. 37). She argues that, until there are Black women working in publishing and criticism, there will only be a filter on the representation of Black women's experiences and their fictions; an unavoidably misleading filter.[30]

The role of autobiographical elements in *Whole* is clearly significant, as many of Nichols's comments in interview reveal. There is also a marked recurrence of incidents and characters in her writing. Thus, for example, the events described in 'Be a Butterfly' (*FBW* 49) appear in an earlier form in *Whole* (*WMS* 8–9). Similarly, 'Miss Sheila/ chocolate queen of dih rundown/ tumbledown tenement yard' in 'Mystery' (*LTLW* 51) is clearly based on the same individual as the Miss Sheila of *Whole*. (See *WMS* 42–3.) Both women are shrouded in mystery, rumoured to have thrown acid in the faces of their lovers; both have left to live in America, only to return to the same men and the same yards; and both are believed to have obeah powers.

Early on in the novel, in one of a series of impressionistic flashbacks to Gem's childhood in Highdam, before the move to Georgetown, Gem remembers 'Standing in sunlight water and watching the dark moving shapes of the fish below' (*WMS* 29). In her introduction to her contribution to *A Caribbean Dozen* (1994), Nichols recalls her 'small-girl days [spent] in a country village on the east coast of Guyana' and reveals that her 'most treasured memory is of myself, around the age of six, standing calf-deep in goldish-brown water, watching fish go by just below the sunlit surface'.[31] Clearly, the childhood experiences focalized by Gem in *Whole* are closely linked to Nichols's own. Indeed, in a 1988 interview, Nichols admitted:

A lot of my childhood is in *A Whole of a Morning Sky*. I was reading a review of the book and wondering whether it wouldn't have worked better as a complete autobiography. I think that was one of the difficulties I found with the novel, because I wasn't being completely autobiographical ... I was being autobiographical to a large extent, but at the same time creating fictional characters too, dimly based on people I had known. So I was battling with the two worlds. (MB 17)

The idea of 'battling with two worlds' is an important one. In this interview Nichols is referring to the world of 'reality' versus that of fiction, but the phrase also has resonances for the migrant writer who must reconstruct 'home' from memory and the imagination.[32]

There are other clearly autobiographical elements to the novel. Clara Walcott, Gem's mother in *Whole*, closely resembles Nichols's description of her own mother as a

warm, intelligent, loving woman who was full of stories, anecdotes and songs from her own childhood. People loved being around her and I can't remember a single day when our home wasn't visited by some friend, neighbour or relative who had dropped in 'just fuh minute' but ended up staying hours. (HT 296)

Archie Walcott, Gem's father, is similarly a headmaster 'inspired by' Nichols's own headmaster father (HT 298). Nichols has spoken in interview of her father as a 'more private and reticent [figure, who] didn't welcome as many people present in our house all the time' (HT 296) but who provided her with the means to access a written literary tradition which complemented the mainly oral, communal matrix of creativity of her mother's world. Nichols recalls:

As a child, at home, with lot of books, I was a regular book hound. My father ... managed to get box of old books from the Public Free Library from time to time for his school and would keep some of these for his own and our reading.

My early exposure to poetry was very much in the English tradition, which would have been the norm in any British colony. Through our school text books, West Indian and Royal Readers, I was thrown into contact with 'The boy stood on the burning deck, whence all but he had fled'. But curled safely between the pages of discarded library books I also discovered the soulful weariness of the home-ward-plodding ploughman whose heartful sadness I identified with completely; the magic and mystery of Christina Rossetti's *Goblin Market*; and a little later, Shakespeare's beautiful sonnets. These to my young ears were the music of poetry. (HT 296–7)

Nichols's fascination with these particular texts suggests just how far the literary standards of the colonizer were internalized by the colonized via the colonial educational system. However, it also testifies to the ways in which the idealized and imaginary worlds of such texts could provide the young colonial subject with an alternative textual universe to that of the authoritative narratives of history, law and realism controlled by the colonizer.[33]

Like Gem, Nichols and her family moved from the country to the capital city, Georgetown, when she was still relatively young (8 years old). The Walcotts arrive in the city in the election year of 1960 and Gem, like Nichols, is able to observe the tumultuous societal and national changes afoot in Guyana immediately before Independence. As Evelyn O'Callaghan notes, 'most of the text is taken up with [the Walcott family's] integration into urban society and the *dis*integration of the city due to political and racial tribalism' (EO 82).

The wealth of correspondences between events in Georgetown in 1950s and 1960s Guyana and those in the city in *Whole of a Morning Sky*[34] lead O'Callaghan to view Nichols's text as a 'thinly-fictionalized memoir of Guyanese social history between the early 1950s and the mid-1960s' (EO 82). Indeed, Nichols has spoken explicitly of 'the setting of the novel and the particular political upheavals of the time [as being] . . . very much part of our political history. In the early sixties the country was in complete civil war really, so lots of things I remember vividly' (MB 17). She acknowledges that she used 'Gem as a means of providing a kind of oblique commentary on the actual events of the time' (MB 17), but stresses that her real concern was 'with the family living through that experience and the characters that fascinated me as a child whom I knew, like the East Indian woman [Mrs Lall in *WMS*] – she really was my neighbour' (MB 17).

O'Callaghan reads *Whole of a Morning Sky* in relation to the first of the novel's epigraphs, an extract from fellow Guyanese

Martin Carter's poem 'Good Friday, 1962'. O'Callaghan suggests that a reading of the lines in the epigraph (as opposed to Carter's poem as a whole) reveals a positive construction of 'violent social change as a glorious upheaval' and a view of revolution as a unifying and transformative process, that works in some specifically gendered ways ('transforms emasculated 'clerks' into heroic 'men' (EO 82). In contrast:

> The prose narrative which follows can be read as an ironic counterpoint to the extract (*not* the whole poem), demonstrating the incongruity of its embedded sentiments. Filtered through the consciousness of the powerless (mostly women) who are caught 'in the crossfire', violent political upheaval – whether state-sanctioned war or popularly sanctioned revolution – emerges as inimical to human life, and unjustified whatever its ideological motivation. (EO 82–3)

O'Callaghan goes on to suggest that the novel as a whole 'picks up key motifs in the excerpt and subverts their emotional appeal by re-contextualization' (EO 83). Central to her reading is the idea of double vision, as reflected in the double narrative perspective and the shifts between the first and third person in the text.

The title of O'Callaghan's study of West Indian women's fiction is simultaneously a critical approach of her own devising. Her coinage of the term 'woman version' derives from the musical term 'dub version', which originated in the Jamaican reggae deejaying tradition. A dub version is created when the deejay takes a master track (in literature the obvious analogy is a master narrative or discourse) and adds new elements (spoken or musical) so 'that something entirely new is created' but 'the original ... remains "recognizably there" on the dub' (EO 11). In her introduction to *Woman Version*, O'Callaghan thus suggests:

> that we approach [West Indian women's writing] ... as a kind of remix or dub version, which utilises elements of the 'master tape' of Caribbean literary discourse (combining, stretching, modifying them in new ways); announces a gendered perspective; adds individual styles of 'talk over'; enhances or omits tracks depending on desired effect; and generally alters by recontextualization to create a unique literary entity. (EO 11)

111

For O'Callaghan *Whole of a Morning Sky* operates as just such a 'woman version' in that it interrogates (dominant narratives of) Guyanese social and national history from a gendered perspective and ultimately discredits violence as the only means to 'social liberation' (EO 84). Nichols makes use of 'parodic, subversive strateg[ies]' to undermine the authority of male figures, 'those who lead the state, the political parties, the schools, the churches' (EO 87).

Even Archie Walcott, Gem's father, is displaced from his former position of authority in the Highdam community as local headmaster and head of the Walcott household. He is now in Georgetown, not Highdam, and is retired from work. In this position, he finds himself having to fit into the well-established rhythms of his wife Clara's days. He is also, crucially, a newcomer in the city, possessing none of her immense social skills and therefore unable to build new networks of friends and associates like her. Even Conrad, Archie's one old friend living in the city, gradually assumes a more central role in the Walcott household than Archie himself, as a reassuring, informing presence with whom Gem forms a close, affectionate bond, as a kind of substitute father-figure.[35]

However, it is the novel's 'woman-centredness' and its emphasis on what O'Callaghan terms 'communality, corporeality and domesticity' (EO 90)[36] which enable her to argue that it is a 'woman version' of the overwhelmingly male-authored history of this period. Nichols's novel is seen as a kind of gendered revisioning which tells Guyanese 'national history ... from the domestic centre "outwards"' (EO 94). In such a reading, the stories of female characters such as Ivy Payne become not incidental to the narrative but central to it. Nichols's novel reminds us that gendered narratives and experiences (and the difference they make) matter. The tumultuous events unfolding in Georgetown impact on Ivy's life in very different ways to that of Archie or Conrad, for example. Moreover, such stories need to be told, for they are not necessarily accounted for in the more visible chartings of the political and economic unrest and racial tensions of this time. Ultimately, the novel suggests possibilities for new ways of relating, inscribing in the domestic arena a tolerance and a bridging of races and cultures which is woefully absent and seemingly impossible in the public sphere. As Jana Gohrish has argued in a different context, Nichols's concern with 'racial and cultural hybridity . . . remain[s] embedded in her preoccupation with gender' (JG 151).

6

Conclusion: Border Crossings and Hybrid Futures

The hybridized quality of much of Nichols's writing is not just a matter of her positioning as a 'writer across two worlds'. It is also a matter of different kinds of border crossings in her work, for example between different registers, styles and genres. Thus, for example, *Whole of a Morning Sky* is comprised of sections of both lyrical prose poetry and those which are narrated in a more straightforwardly realist style. Similarly, *i is a long memoried woman* is characterized by border crossings between the oral and scribal traditions, and this enables Nichols to integrate oral traditional resources such as work-song, prayer, incantation and invocation into her poem cycle. Another permutation of border crossing in her work is of course the shift between different registers and the 'fusing' or 'merging' of creole and standard English. Her writing draws upon European myth and literature but also a rich vein of Caribbean, African and other cultural resources. In this way she can be seen as a writer who 'lives and writes across the margins of different traditions and cultural universes'.[1] In each case, her position at the border, the liminal space, allows her to collapse restrictive binaries and to achieve a more creatively imagined synthesis in her work.

In the introduction to this study it was also argued that it is more productive to read Nichols's writing in terms of a series of 'border crossings', rather than seeing her 'Britishness' and 'Caribbeanness' as dual affiliations simplistically opposed. To cross borders is, in the words of Avtar Brah, to move 'across shifting cultural, religious and linguistic boundaries . . . [to]

journey across geographical and psychic borders' (AB 204). It is also, as a number of feminist critics have argued, to recognize that the subject is simultaneously 'situated within gendered spaces of class, racism, ethnicity, sexuality, age' (CD 204). Clearly, Nichols's work combines border crossings of both kinds. It examines what it means and has meant for the African slave and the more recent Caribbean migrant, to undergo their respective geographical, spiritual and psychic journeys. It also considers the boundaries of race, class and gender which are part of the 'everyday, lived experience' of being a black woman in Britain. But how has this border crossing been theorized? One response has been the theoretical concept of cultural hybridity, a concept most closely associated with postcolonial theory, and with the work of Homi Bhabha.

In this chapter, the concept of hybridity is considered in terms of its possible usefulness in a reading of Nichols's writing. Although no major postcolonial study of Nichols's work exists at the time of writing this study, a number of shorter critical readings have been produced. In her essay 'Gender and Hybridity in Contemporary Caribbean Poetry', Jana Gohrisch combines insights from Bhabha's theories of hybridity with theories of creolization in the writing of Barbadian-born poet, historian and critic Kamau Brathwaite. In this way, she is able to account for both the global and the indigenous manifestations of postcolonial theory, keeping open the possibility of locating Nichols's work within a specifically Caribbean as well as wider theoretical context.

As is often the case with Caribbean literature, some of the key critical and theoretical voices are also those of prominent creative figures. In the case of Caribbean theories of hybridity, they include critical writing by Brathwaite, Wilson Harris and Derek Walcott.[2] Gohrisch contrasts Brathwaite's regionally based 'historical investigation into practised hybridity' (GH 140) in his seminal study *The Development of Creole Society in Jamaica 1770–1820* (1971) with 'the current international debate on hybridity, which seems to be dominated by poststructuralist methodology in the wake of Homi Bhabha' (JG 140). She observes that Brathwaite recognizes in his theory of creolization that 'hybridity is closely connected with the issue of gender' (JG 155) but that gender issues remain relatively undeveloped in his critical/theoretical writing. Bhabha occupies a special place in her interrogation of gender bias and marginalization of gender issues in these male theorists' work, as he is one of a growing number of postcolonial critics who seem (whether deliberately or by default due to the level of abstraction of their writing) 'increasingly concerned with the role of the intellectual (male) migrant in Western societies as a mediator between cultures' (JG 140). For Gohrisch, Nichols's poetry is a corrective to this bias since it explores hybridity as a historical process rather than a theoretical abstraction. More importantly, as this study has argued, it refocuses attention on the crucial 'contribution of the (female) African slaves and their descendants to the development of racial and cultural hybridity in the Caribbean' (JG 142). However, Gohrisch does not go as far as to argue that Nichols's creative writing might itself theorize these issues in new ways.

For Bhabha, the migrant occupies an ambivalent, uncertain, even contradictory, space on the borders between cultures, languages, nations. Rather than reading this as a position of loss and cultural dilution (a notion which Bhabha would not subscribe to anyhow since the idea of pure, fixed or essentialized races, cultures or nations is one he is at pains to deconstruct), Bhabha argues that the migrant occupies a privileged space. This is precisely because 'Cultural identity always emerges in this contradictory and ambivalent space' (JM 118), what Bhabha terms 'the third space of enunciation'. As John McLeod suggests:

> Standing at the border, the migrant is empowered to intervene actively in the transmission of cultural inheritance or 'tradition' (of both the home and host land) rather than passively accept its venerable customs and ... wisdom. He or she can question, refashion or mobilise received ideas. The migrant is empowered as an agent of change ... (JM 218–19)

Something of this possibility is captured in Nichols's comments that 'difference, diversity and unpredictability make [her] tick' (LN 98) and her observation that:

> Caribbean people on the whole ... have that fluidity about them in that they can connect easily ... with other cultures and people because we have all these different cultures ... [within us] (PGN)

116

Her point echoes Gohrisch's notion of a 'practised hybridity' in arguing that because Caribbean people are already inherently hybrid (that is, largely composed of migrant peoples from a number of different racial backgrounds), their culture a thoroughly creolized one, they are able to conceptualize their identities as being more fluid, provisional and mobile. This concept of the hybrid subject is one that Bhabha would recognize and endorse, not least because it provides a way 'of thinking beyond exclusionary, fixed, binary notions of identity based on ideas of rootedness and cultural, racial and national purity' (JM 219). In this way 'the concept of hybridity has proved very important for Diaspora peoples, and indeed many others too' (JM 219).

Several poems by Nichols seem appropriate in this context. In 'sunris' the protagonist identifies herself as 'a hybrid-dreamer' as well as an 'An ancestral-believer' (S 52). She refers to 'the intricacies of [her] blood' and makes the thoroughly creolized and creolizing challenge to men of all races 'to come out to tasteup mih race' (S 53). 'Tapestry' (LTLW 57) celebrates the Caribbean subject as racially hybrid:

> An African countenance here
> A European countenance there
> An Amerindian cast of cheek
> An Asiatic turn of eye . . .

However, the poem also suggests hybridity as a position in which change can be effected and new forms and modes of identities established, thus the claiming of nation language as 'the tongue's salty accommodation'. This inherently creative potential is also reflected in the poem's images of ancestry as a 'tapestry . . . bloodstained prints . . . scatterlinks'. 'Tapestry' comes at the end of the collection Lazy Thoughts and yet it is a poem which resists closure. Indeed, it anticipates the more sustained exploration of cultural hybridity in 'sunris'.

In 'Wings' (S 77–9) Nichols takes the familiar Caribbean notion of roots and rootedness and suggests an alternative aesthetic of flight. The specific cultural meanings of the trope of flight as it appears in spirituals and slave narratives, as well as more contemporary writings within an African-American tradition, has received considerable critical attention. Nichols alludes to this belief in the transmigration of souls (that the soul would take flight and return to Africa when a slave died) in the lines:

> But wasn't it wings
> That made our ancestors
> Climb the airy staircase
> Whenever they contemplated
> Rock and hard place

(S 78)

However, she explores the notion of flight more widely, suggesting various permutations and metaphorical possibilities. Thus 'our own wilful wings' stand accused of 'still taking us into migratory-pull/ still taking us into homing-instinct' (S 78), conjuring up similar images of the diasporic West Indian endlessly criss-crossing the Atlantic to that in the epigraph by Pauline Melville to chapter 5. However, the main possibility of 'Wings' is one of transcendence from fixity and the past, itself a quintessentially hybrid gesture. Nichols describes herself and her fellow West Indians as:

> Root-lovers
> Root grounders
> Root-worshippers . . .
>
> Always an inward yearning
> For . . . lost Africas, Indias . . .
> The love-tugging land
> Of our immediate birthmothers.
> Past more poignant
> Than any future.

(S 77)

In the process of 'constantly counting/ our sea-chest of losses', of being 'old hoarding mourners', she suggests West Indians have 'forg[otten] the other end . . . the imperishable gift of our wings' (S 78). The remaining stanzas of the poem compose a picture of West Indian peoples and their culture in fragments, as if viewed from the air. The language of this part of the poem is sanctifying and benedictory. As such it is reminiscent of Derek Walcott's *The Bounty*, or the benedictory tones of George Campbell's 'Holy'. In this new aesthetic of wings, Nichols

118

finds the fullest expression of cultural hybridity as a space of boundless possibilities. Indeed, the poem demonstrates how 'hybrid identities are never total and complete in themselves ... Instead they remain perpetually in motion, pursuing errant and unpredictable routes, open to change and reinscription' (JM) One can only hope that Nichols's future writing will continue to be thus: thoroughly mobile and unfixed, following its own 'errant and unpredictable routes, open to change and reinscription'.

Notes

CHAPTER 1. CHARTING THE TERRAIN

1. See below in this chapter and bibliography for details of anthologies which include poems by Nichols.
2. These are not necessarily the same thing as Gina Wisker's 1993 study, *Black Women's Writing* testifies with its inclusion of analyses of African-American, African and South African writers alongside Black British and Caribbean writers such as Nichols.
3. See Sarah Lawson Welsh, 'Critical Myopia and Black British Literature: Reassessing the Literary Contribution of the Post-Windrush generation(s)', *Kunapipi*, 20:1 (1998), 132–42.
4. These included *A Dangerous Knowing* (1985); *Purple and Green: Poems by Women Poets* (1985); *Watchers and Seekers* (1987); *Ain't I A Woman!* (1987); *Charting the Journey* (1988); *Her True-True Name* (1989); *Creation Fire* (1990) and *Daughters of Africa* (1992).
5. George Lamming, *The Pleasures of Exile* (London: Allison & Busby, 1984), 214.
6. For more detail on this and other periods from a Caribbean perspective, see decade introductions in Alison Donnell and Sarah Lawson Welsh (eds), *The Routledge Reader in Caribbean Literature* (London and New York: 1996); for a black British perspective, see James Procter *Writing Black Britain 1948–1998* (Manchester: Manchester University Press: 2000).
7. Even after independence, the literary curriculum of the West Indian education system was still dominated by texts from the English literary canon, and very few texts by indigenous writers were taught (if at all). This well-documented fact, was just one of the legacies of colonial rule in the Caribbean. Significantly however, a number of Caribbean writers, including Derek Walcott, have also spoken of the enormous benefits of their 'sound colonial education'.

8. See Anne Walmsley, *The Caribbean Artist's Movement, 1966–72* (London: New Beacon Books, 1992), for more detailed discussion of CAM's role in fostering Caribbean literary creativity.
9. See below in this chapter for a definition of these terms and an introduction to language politics in the Caribbean.
10. Certain important qualifications to Berry's statement do need to be made. That 'suitable work from women writers had not been submitted or found' (Introduction, *Barefoot Traveller* (2nd edn; Walton-on-Thames: Thomas Nelson & Sons, 1981), 6) does not necessarily mean that it did not exist in Britain before the early 1980s. Crucially Berry does not define what he means by 'suitable work' and it is not clear how sustained was his search for such writing.
11. Linton Kwesi Johnson's 'Di Great Insohreckshan' was the single poem included in this anthology.
12. 1998 marked the fiftieth anniversary of the *SS Empire Windrush's* arrival at Tilbury Docks, with 492 Jamaican passengers aboard destined for work and new lives in Britain. Although this was not in fact the first arrival of West Indians in Britain in this period, it has become enshrined in popular mythology as the starting point for the post (Second World) war migration of thousands of West Indians to Britain.
13. 'Interview: Linton Kwesi Johnson Talks to Burt Caesar', *Critical Quarterly*, 38:4 (Winter 1996), 72.
14. See also Lauretta Ngcobo (ed.), *Let It Be Told* (London: Virago, 1988): 'As a writer I feel strongly multi-cultural and very Caribbean' (p. 96).
15. In this formulation, I am indebted to Carole Boyce Davies's proposal that: 'Black women's writing ... should be read as a series of boundary crossings and not as a fixed, geographically, ethnically or nationally bound category of writing' (*Black Women, Writing and Identity* (London and New York: Routledge, 1994), 4).
16. Avtar Brah, *Cartographies of Diaspora* (London and New York: Routledge, 1996), 198.
17. Sheila Allen, 'Race, Ethnicity and Gender', in Haleh Afshar and Mary Maynard (eds), *The Dynamics of 'Race' and Gender* (London and Bristol, PA: Taylor and Francis, 1994), 100.
18. James Clifford, 'Travelling Cultures', in Lawrence Grossberg, Cary Nelson and Paula Treichler (eds), *Cultural Studies* (London and New York: Routledge, 1992), 99.
19. See Sarah Lawson Welsh, ' "(Un)belonging Citizens, Unmapped Territory": Black Immigration and British identity in the Post-1945 Period', in Stuart Murray (ed.), *Not On Any Map: Essays on Postcoloniality and Cultural Nationalism*, 43–66, for further detail.

20. Merle Hodge, 'Challenges of the Struggle for Sovereignty', in Selwyn R. Cudjoe (ed.), *Caribbean Women Writers: Essays from the First International Conference* (Wellesley, MA: Calaloux, 1990), 204.

21. See Paule Marshall, in Robyn R. Warhol and Diane Price Herndl (eds), *Feminisms: An Anthology of Literary Theory and Criticism* (New Brunswick, NJ: Rutgers University Press, 1991), 334.

22. See Morgan Dalphinis's *Caribbean & African Languages: Social History, Language, Literature and Education* (London: Karia Press, 1985), 85–96 and 165–72, for further reading on the African basis of Caribbean creoles and African influences in Caribbean literature.

23. David Dabydeen, 'On Writing Slave Song', *Commonwealth*, 8:2 (1989), 46–50, quoted in Sarah Lawson Welsh, 'Experiments in Brokenness: The Creative Use of Creole in David Dabydeen's *Slave Song*', in Donnell and Welsh (eds), *Routledge Reader in Caribbean Literature*, 423–4.

24. Kamau Brathwaite, *History of the Voice*, (London: New Beacon, 1984), 13.

25. Ibid.

26. Mervyn Morris, 'On Reading Louise Bennett, Seriously', *Jamaica Journal*, 1:1 (1967), 69–74; repr. in Donnell and Welsh (eds), *Routledge Reader in Caribbean Literature*, 194–7.

27. Peter Parker (ed.), *The Reader's Companion to Twentieth Century Writers* (Oxford: Helicon, 1995), 543.

28. Jamaica Kincaid, *A Small Place* (London: Virago, 1988), 14.

29. See chapter 2 for a fuller account of the Hottentot Venus. For further reading, see also Sander Gilman, 'Black Bodies, White Bodies: Toward an Iconography of Female Sexuality in Nineteenth-century Art, Medicine and Literature', in Henry Louis Gates (ed.), *'Race', Writing and Difference* (Chicago and London: Chicago University Press: 1985).

30. I am indebted to Ruth Robbins for this useful observation on the function of humour in Nichols's work.

CHAPTER 2: FEMINIST READINGS

1. Frantz Fanon, *Black Skin: White Masks*, trans. Charles Lam Markmann (London: Pluto Press, 1986), 231–2.

2. Robyn R. Warhol and Diane Price Herndl (eds), *Feminisms: An Anthology of Literary Theory and Criticism* (New Brunswick, NJ: Rutgers University Press, 1991), 332.

3. Lorde delivered 'Uses of the Erotic: The Erotic as Power' at the Fourth Berkshire Conference on the History of Women, at Mount

Holyoke College, USA. on 25 August 1978. It was published as a pamphlet by Out and Out Books, then as *Uses of the Erotic: The Erotic as Power* in 1981, and reprinted in Lorde's *Sister Outsider: Essays and Speeches* (Freedom, CA: Crossing Press, 1984), 53–9.

4. These include: Maggie Butcher's 'Interview with Grace Nichols' in *Wasafiri*, 8 (1988), 17–20; Kwame Dawes's interview with Grace Nichols in his *Talk Yuh Talk: Interviews with Anglophone Caribbean Poets* (Charlottesville and London: University Press of Virginia, 2000), 135–47; Elfi Bettinger's 'Grace Nichols's "Sugar Cane"': A Post-Colonial and Feminist Perspective', in *Anglistik und Englischunterricht*, 53 (1994), 117–27, and Jana Gohrisch's 'Gender and Hybridity in Contemporary Caribbean Poetry', in Raimund Borgmeier, Herbert Grabes and Andreas H. Jucker (eds), *Anglistentag 1997 Giessen: Proceedings* (Trier: WVT, 1998), 139–56. Exceptionally, Isabel Hoving devotes a whole chapter to Nichols's use of orality, focalization and creole language politics in her recent book *In Praise of New Travellers: Reading Caribbean Migrant Women's Writing* (Stanford: Stanford University Press, 2001), but even she chooses to focus not primarily on Nichols's poetry but on her novel *Whole of a Morning Sky*.

5. Denise de Caires Narain reviews these readings in chapter 4 of her *Contemporary Caribbean Women's Poetry: Making Style* (London and New York: Routledge, 2002), 194–6.

6. Lauretta Ngcobo makes a similar point in a black British context in her editor's note to *Let It Be Told* (London: Virago Press, 1988): 'We have been writing for a long time; it is now that these writings are beginning to come out in the open' (p. ix).

7. Françoise Lionnet, *Postcolonial Representations: Women, Literature, Identity* (Ithaca and London: Cornell University Press, 1995), 27.

8. Lloyd Brown, Introduction to Erika Sollish Smilowitz and Roberta Quarles Knowles (eds), *Critical Issues in West Indian Literature* (Parkersburg, IA: Caribbean Books, 1984), 3.

9. Patricia Mohammed, 'Towards Indigenous Feminist Theorizing in the Caribbean', in Patricia Mohammed (ed.), *Rethinking Caribbean Difference*, a special issue of *Feminist Review*, 59 (1998), 6.

10. The most famous of these is Audre Lorde's 'The Master's Tools Will Never Dismantle the Master's House', which Lorde delivered at a number of academic conferences, including the MLA's 'Lesbian and Literature Panel' in Chicago in 1977 and 'The Personal and Political Panel' at the Second Sex Conference in the United States 1979. In this piece, Lorde identifies herself as a black feminist lesbian poet and speaks out against the 'absence of any consideration of lesbian consciousness or the consciousness

of third world women' in certain 'academic feminist circles' and the wider silencing of the input of 'black and third-world women, and lesbians' in 'discussion of feminist theory at this time' (Cherrie Moraga and Gloria Anzaldua (eds), *This Bridge Called My Back: Writings by Radical Women of Color* (New York: Kitchen Table, Women of Color Press, 1983), 98, 100). The same 'battle against silence' (Mary Eagleton, *Working with Feminist Criticism* (Oxford: Blackwell, 1996), 23) and urge to white 'academic feminists' to enter into dialogue with women of colour and black feminists underlines Lorde's 'Open Letter to Mary Daly' (repr. in Moraga and Anzaldua (eds), *This Bridge Called My Back*, 94–7).

11. F. N. Simmonds, 'Difference, Power and Knowledge: Black Women in Academia', in H. Hinds et al. (eds), *Working Out: New Directions for Women's Studies* (London: Falmer Press, 1992), 52.

12. Barbara Christian, 'The Race for Theory', *Cultural Critique*, 6 (1987), repr. in Bill Ashcroft, Gareth Griffiths and Helen Tiffin (eds), *The Post-Colonial Studies Reader* (London and New York: Routledge, 1995), 457.

13. See, for example, 'Ode to My Bleed' (*LTLW* 24), 'My Black Triangle' (*LTLW* 25), 'On Poems and Crotches' (*LTLW* 16) and 'Spell Against Too Much Male White Power' (*LTLW* 18–19).

14. American feminist Elaine Showalter defines *écriture féminine* as 'the inscription of the feminine body and female difference in language and text' ('Feminist Criticism in the Wilderness', in Elaine Showalter (ed.), *The New Feminist Criticism* (London: Virago, 1986), 249. British feminist Ruth Robbins defines Cixous's 'project' as a search for 'a writing that could adequately represent female/feminine positions in relation to culture'. Other attempts to define *l'écriture feminine* resort to a number of recurrent metaphors (used in the writings of the theorists themselves) including the idea of 'writing the body'.

15. Ruth Robbins, for example, calls Cixous's project 'Utopian' (*Literary Feminisms* (Basingstoke: Macmillan, 2000), 168).

16. Gabriele Griffin, 'Writing the Body: Reading Joan Riley, Grace Nichols and Ntozake Shange', in Gina Wisker (ed.), *Black Women's Writing* (Houndmills: Macmillan Press, 1993), 33.

17. Gudrun Webhofer, '*Identity*' in the Poetry of Grace Nichols and Lorna Goodison* (Lewiston, NY: Edwin Mellen Press, 1996), 16.

18. Margaret Homans, '"Women of Color" Writers and Feminist Theory', in Robyn R. Warhol and Diane Price Herndl (eds), *Feminisms: An Anthology of Literary Theory and Criticism* (Basingstoke: Macmillan, 1997), 417.

19. Ibid., 407.

20. Valerie Smith, 'Black Feminist Theory and the Representation of the "Other"', in Cheryl A. Wall ed., *Changing Our Own Words: Essays on Criticism, Theory, and Writing by Black Women* (London and New York: Routledge, 1989), 45.
21. Ibid., 45.
22. 'My race began as the sea began,/ with no nouns, and with no horizon, with pebbles under my tongue,/ with a different fix on the stars' (Derek Walcott, *Collected Poems* (New York: Noonday Press, 1988), 305).
23. Derek Walcott, 'The Muse of History', in Orde Coombs (ed.), *Is Massa Day Dead?* (New York: Doubleday/Anchor Press, 1974), repr. in Donnell and Lawson Welsh (eds), *Routledge Reader in Caribbean Literature*, 356–7.
24. 'Jou'vert', in Kamau Brathwaite, *The Arrivants* (Oxford: Oxford University Press, 1986), 270.
25. Nichols has spoken of Nanny as 'the Jamaican rebel heroine who played a great role in fighting for freedom for her people, for she established the first big [Maroon] colony [of runaway slaves] in the hills of Jamaica' (BBC Radio 3 dramatization of *i is a long memoried woman*, 8 November 1991). As Louis James notes: ' "Nanny" (or "Ni") as a resistance leader against the British in the early 1700s has provided a focus for militancy in West Indian women's writing, bringing into prominence a figure whose name remains in the ruined "Nanny Town" concealed deep in the Jamaican mountains, but previously shadowy in Jamaican folk history. While male leaders such as Cudjoe were renowned principally as warriors, Nanny has been celebrated as being also a priestess and cultural organiser of the Maroon community. Goodison's poem "Nanny" celebrates her transmission of healing arts from Africa ... Nanny lies at the heart of the novel *Abeng* (1984) by the Jamaican-born novelist Michelle Cliff' (*Caribbean Literature in English* (London and New York: Longman, 1999), 206–7).
26. See Mohammed, 'Towards Indigenous Feminist Theorizing in the Caribbean', 6–33, for a discussion of some of these issues.
27. Paraskevi Papaleonida, ' "holding my beads in my hand": Dialogue, Synthesis and power in the Poetry of Jackie Kay and Grace Nichols', in Vicki Bertram (ed.), *Kicking Daffodils* (Edinburgh: Edinburgh University Press, 1997), 125–39.
28. Vicki Bertram, 'Muscling In: A Study of Contemporary Women Poets and English Poetic Tradition', University of York, DPhil dissertation, 1992, 55.
29. Two important precursors to this and other poems dealing with the fat black woman's response to prescribed notions of size and

beauty in Britain, are 'Cinema Eyes' and 'Kinky Hair Blues' by Jamaican poet, Una Marson, first published in 1937. Both poems are reprinted in Donnell and Lawson Welsh (eds), *Routledge Reader in Caribbean Literature*, 137–40.

30. For example, Gudrun Webhofer notes the use of this strategy in 'The Assertion' (*FBW* 8). See Webhofer, *'Identity'*, 21. It is also found in poems such as 'Web of Kin' (*IMW* 8–9) and most notably in 'Of Course When They Ask for Poems About the "Realities" of Black Woman' (*LTLW* 52–4).

31. 'Spell Against Too Much Male Power' is the title of another Nichols poem from *Lazy Thoughts of a Lazy Woman* (pp. 18–19).

32. Hilary Beckles, 'Historicizing Slavery in West Indian Feminisms', in Mohammed (ed.), *Rethinking Caribbean Difference*, 37.

33. Patricia Morton quoted in Beckles, 'Historicizing Slavery', 37.

34. Baartman was born in 1789 in the Khosian tribal homelands of South Africa. After campaigning by Nelson Mandela's post-apartheid government, her remains were handed back to South Africa by France in a symbolic gesture of reconciliation in 2002. She has since been honoured and ceremonially buried in the homeland from whence she was taken in 1819. This is also the subject of a longer poem by Jackie Kay, 'Hottentot Venus', in *Penguin Modern Poets*, 8 (London: Penguin, 1996), 46–7.

35. I am indebted to Isobel Armstrong for this pertinent observation.

36. See chapter 3 for a more detailed reading of this poem.

37. See Jan Nederve Pieterse, *White on Black: Images of Africa and Blacks in Western Popular Culture* (New Haven and London: Yale University Press, 1992).

38. I am indebted to Ruth Robbins for suggesting the basis of some of the points in this final section.

CHAPTER 3. EPIC JOURNEYING I: *I IS A LONG MEMORIED WOMAN*

1. BBC Radio 3 adaptation of *i is*. The lines Nichols refers to are from 'Web of Kin' (*ILMW* 8–9): 'Even in dreams I will submerge myself/ swimming like one possessed/ back and forth across that course/ strewing it with sweet smelling/flowers/one for every-one who made the journey'.

2. Vicki Bertram ed. *Kicking Daffodils: Twentieth-Century Women Poets* (Edinburgh: Edinburgh University Press, 1997), 1.

3. Importantly it is also a recurrent trope in black women's writing, as Susan Willis notes with reference to mainly African-American

women writers in 'Black Women Writers: Taking a Critical Perspective', in Gayle Greene and Coppelia Kahn (eds), *Making a Difference: Feminist Literary Criticism* (London and New York, Routledge: 1991), 219–26.

4. *Sunris* is the collection; 'sunris' the title poem.

5. In this context, the following comment by Kamau Brathwaite is illuminating: 'In the Caribbean, whether it be African or Amerindian, the recognition of an ancestral relationship with the folk or aboriginal culture involves the artist and participant in a journey into the past and hinterland which is at the same time a movement of possession into present and future. Through this movement of possession we become ourselves, truly our own creators, discovering word for object, image for the Word.' ('Timehri', in Donnell and Lawson Welsh, *Routledge Reader in Caribbean Literature*, 350).

6. Liz Yorke, *Impertinent Voices* (London and New York: Routledge, 1991), 16.

7. This is also Nichols's project in 'The Fat Black Woman Composes a Black poem' (*FBW* 16) and 'Black' and 'White' (*S* 10–11).

8. Dennis Walder prefers to term Nichols 'a satirist ... whose manner is sly, brash, exuberant, laid-back and wonderfully economic, refusing cliché while drawing on the myths of old and new world to articulate a complex fluid vision'. Yet he too acknowledges the importance of Nichols's subversion of gender roles when he points out that 'traditionally in English [the satirist is] the male poet's role', *Post-colonial Literatures in English* (Oxford: Blackwell, 1998), 148.

9. See *Slave Song* (Hebden Bridge: Dangaroo, 1984), and especially 'The Sexual Word' in *Coolie Odyssey* (London and Coventry: Hansib & Dangaroo, 1988), 32.

10. Gina Wisker, *Post-Colonial and African-American Women's Writing: A Critical Introduction* (Houndmills and London: Macmillan, 2000), 292.

11. Webhofer records how 'In a public poetry performance (Swansea, April 1995) Grace Nichols explained that the image of the Golden Stool is borrowed from Ashanti mythology. Only the Ashanti King was allowed to sit on it, once a year and for one day only. The stool, according to Nichols, represents the soul of Ashanti nationhood' (*'Identity' in the Poetry of Grace Nichols and Lorna Goodison* (Lewiston, NY: Edwin Mellen Press, 1996), 21). This is supported by Kamau Brathwaite's earlier poem, 'The Golden Stool' which describes how 'down in thunder from his heaven/ Anokye brought the Golden stool' (*Arrivants*, 144).

127

12. Ostriker notes how H.D. called the poem her 'Cantos', thus issuing an 'implicit challenge to Ezra Pound's culturally encyclopaedic *Cantos*', *Stealing the Language: The Emergence of Women's Poetry in America* (London: Women's Press, 1986), 228.
13. See Walder, *Post-colonial Literatures in English*, 147.
14. 'Geopsyche' is a term coined by Brathwaite to refer to the peculiar resonances of a particular place or landscape. As the term suggests, 'geopsyche' combines the sense of geological and psychological characteristics, the mind or spirit of a given place or topography.
15. See 'Omen' (*ILMW* 81–2).
16. Douglas Hall, *The Caribbean Experience* (London and Kingston, Jamaica: Heinemann Educational, 1982), 61. See also C. L. R. James, *The Black Jacobins* (London: Allison & Busby, 1980) for a fuller account of this.
17. Patrick Williams, 'Difficult Subjects: Black British Women's Poetry', in David Murray (ed.), *Literary Theory and Poetry: Extending the Canon* (London: Batsford, 1989), 124–5.
18. Derek Walcott, 'What the Twilight Says', in *Dream on Monkey Mountain and Other Plays* (New York: Farrar, Strauss and Giroux, 1970), 4; repr. in Derek Walcott, *What the Twilight Says: Essays* (London: Faber & Faber, 1998), 3–35.
19. Marlene Nourbese Phillip, 'Dis Place The Space Between', in Lynn Keller and Cristanne Miller (eds), *Feminist Measures: Soundings in Poetry and Theory* (Ann Arbor: University of Michigan Press, 1994), 289.
20. See Derek Walcott, 'What the Twilight Says', 'The Muse of History' and 'The Antilles: Fragments of Epic Memory', in Walcott, *What the Twilight Says*, 3–84.
21. A number of other black women's texts feature such acts of infanticide, intended to liberate the child from a life of slavery, most famously Toni Morrison's *Beloved* (London: Chatto & Windus, 1987). There are also a number of contemporary documents which testify to this kind of punishment, most notably the engravings of slaves in John Stedman's *Narrative of a Five Years' Expedition against the revolted Negroes of Surinam* (1796).
22. Barbara Bush, 'Towards Emancipation: Slave Women and Resistance to Coercive Labour Regimes in the British West Indian Colonies, 1790–1838', *Slavery and Abolition*, 5 (December 1984), 228.
23. *History of the Voice* (London: New Beacon Books, 1984), 7. Brathwaite is alluding here to the contemporary creoles or 'nation language' used by contemporary Caribbean writers.

24. I am indebted to Ruth Robbins for this useful observation.
25. See also David Dabydeen's *Slave Song* for similar poems of female slave resistance.
26. Bush, 'Towards Emancipation', 228.
27. In Caribbean folklore 'Old Higue' or 'Ol' Higue' is an evil spirit which takes the form of a haggard old woman.
28. Introduction to Paula Burnett (ed.), *The Penguin Book of Caribbean Verse in English* (Harmondsworth, Middlesex: Penguin), xxvii.
29. In *Purple and Green: Poems by 33 Woman Poets* (London: Riveline Grapheme Press, 1985), 117.
30. Wisker, *Post-Colonial and African-American Women's Writing*, 292.
31. 'Narah pains' are abdominal pains often linked to twisting of the intestines. It is believed that massage can help both pain and twisting.
32. C. L. Innes, 'Accent and Identity: Women Poets of Many Parts', in James Acheson and Romana Huk (eds), *Contemporary British Poetry: Essays in Theory and Criticism* (New York: State University of New York Press, 1996), 323.
33. See, for example, Elfi Bettinger's 'Grace Nichols's "Sugar Cane": a Post-Colonial and Feminist Perspective', *Anglistik und Englischunterricht*, 53 (1994), 117–27.
34. In Henry Louis Gates Jr and Nellie Y. McKay (eds), *The Norton Anthology of African American Literature* (New York and London: 1997), 2205–6.
35. In Olive Senior, *Gardening in the Tropics* (Newcastle-upon-Tyne: Bloodaxe, 1994), 131–3. Senior devotes the final section of the collection, entitled 'Mystery', to poems which explore different African Orishas, gods and goddesses in the New World.
36. Louis James, *Caribbean Literature in English* (Harlow, Essex: Longman, 1999), 207.
37. Ibid.
38. Brathwaite, *Arrivants*, 242–3. See also Olive Senior's 'Ogun: God of Iron', in *Gardening in the Tropics*, 119–20.
39. I am indebted to Ruth Robbins for this helpful suggestion.
40. Carole Boyce Davies, *Black Women, Writing and Identity* (London and New York: Routledge, 1994), 163.

CHAPTER 4. EPIC JOURNEYING II: 'SUNRIS'

1. These texts include Trinidadian Earl Lovelace's novel *The Dragon Can't Dance* (1979), Trinidadian Willi Chen's *King of the Carnival and Other Stories* (1988), Hazel Campbell's short stories, *Singerman*

(1991), Barbadian Kamau Brathwaite's 'Caliban', 'Tizzic' and 'Jou'vert' from *Islands* (1969), part of his *Arrivants* trilogy, St Lucian Derek Walcott's ' Mass Man' in *The Gulf* (1969), Nichols's own 'Even tho' (*LTLW* 21) and Guyanese Wilson Harris's challenging and complex novel *Carnival* (1985).

2. The folkloric figure of Papa Bois (literally, 'Father Wood) is half-man, half-beast in appearance with cloven hoofs. He is the keeper of the woods.

3. 'Beyond the Pale', in Margaret Busby (ed.), *Daughters of Africa* (London: Vintage, 1993), 742–3.

4. Brathwaite, *History of the Voice*, 7.

5. See Mikhail Bakhtin, *Rabelais and His World*, trans. Helene Iswoksky (Bloomington: Indian University Press; 1968).

6. Nichols lists some of these herself in her introduction to *Sunris* (*S* 2–3). Chief of these explorations of carnival is Trinidadian Earl Lovelace's novel *The Dragon Can't Dance* (1979). In his novel Lovelace explores the complex tensions between playing 'mas' as an act of faith, a belief in the salvation of this cleansing and unifying ritual of carnival, and 'mas' as play-acting, taking on an assumed (and ultimately false) persona, as well as the pull between the local and the 'foreign', between keeping 'tradition' and the incipient commercialization of carnival. Other Trinidadian explorations of calypso and the role of the calypsonian include short stories: Ian McDonald's 'Jaffo the Calypsonian', Sam Selvon's 'Calypsonian', and Naipaul's 'B. Wordsworth' in his early novel *Miguel Street* (1959). However, it has not been a Trinidadian preserve, as St Lucian Derek Walcott's poem 'The Spoiler's Return', Hazel Campbell's short stories, *Singerman* (1991) and Nichols's 'sunris' testify. Similarly, in the case of steel pan – another vital component of carnival – it has been non-Trinidadians such as Guyanese John Agard in his 'Man to Pan' poems in *Mangoes and Bullets* (1985), Grenadian born Trinidadian resident Abdul Malik in his *Pan Run* sequences I and II from *The Whirlwind* (1988), and Nichols herself in 'sunris', who have explored the poetic possibilities of pan most fully. See also Trinidadian Errol Hill's plays *Ping Pong* (1958), and *Man Better Man* (1964), Marion Patrick Jones's novels *Pan Beat* (1973), and *J'Ouvert Morning* (1976) and Victor Questel's 'Pan Drama', in *Near Mourning Ground* (1979).

7. In *Whole of a Morning Sky*, Archie 'had come to dread those weekends . . . when Ivy Payne held her weekly Saturday night-dances and Sunday picnics . . . with the loud music and rum drinking next door' (*WMS* 120), although Clara hums along and Gem knows 'all the words of the latest calypsos'.

8. Campbell's 'Holy' opens with the lines: 'Holy be the white head of a Negro/ Sacred be the black flax of a black child./ Holy be/ The golden down/ That will stream in the waves of the winds/ And will thin like dispersing clouds' (Donnell and Lawson Welsh (eds), *Routledge Reader in Caribbean Literature*, 143).

9. Earl Lovelace, *The Dragon Can't Dance* (Harlow, Essex: Longman, 1981; orig. pub. 1979), 88.

10. A light-skinned, rusty-complexioned person.

11. Brathwaite, 'Timehri', in Donnell and Lawson Welsh (eds), *Routledge Reader in Caribbean Literature*, 347.

12. The subject of the Jonestown massacre has also been treated by fellow Guyanese writers, Wilson Harris in *Jonestown* (London: Faber & Faber, 1999) and Fred D'Aguiar in *Bill of Rights* (London: Chatto & Windus, 1998).

13. Rachel DuPlessis notes how this 'great Goddess Venus/Isis [also] stands behind [H.D.'s poetry] ... The Goddess, especially her intermingling of sexuality and maternity, of creation and procreation, or writing and eros, is the commanding presence of maternal and erotic/sexual authority who is created in many phases of H.D.'s oeuvre' *H.D. The Career of That Struggle* (Bloomington: Indiana University Press, 1986), 129.

14. In an intriguing parallel, H.D. also used the term 'Hellas' in a note on her early work to refer to her 'nostalgia for a lost [classical] land', adding that it had special significance as Helen was her mother's name (*Oxford Anthology of Poetry*, 1938, 1287; cited in *H.D. The Career of That Struggle*, 14–15).

CHAPTER 5. 'A WRITER ACROSS TWO WORLDS'

1. Pauline Melville, *Shape-Shifter* (London: Women Press, 1990), 149.

2. Fred D'Aguiar, *British Subjects* (Newcastle upon Tyne: Bloodaxe, 1993), 114.

3. Grace Nichols, *The Poetry of Grace Nichols*, 'English File' video, programme 3 in the *Poetry Backpack* series for schools (1997).

4. See also Nichols's 'Emerald Heart' (*LTLW* 41) which also makes reference to this belief.

5. For example: Caryl Phillips's *A State of Independence* (London: Faber, 1986), Amryl Johnson's *Sequins for a Ragged Hem* (London: Virago, 1987), Linton Kwesi Johnson's 'Reggae fi dada', in *Tings an' Times* (Newcastle upon Tyne: Bloodaxe, 1992) and Pauline Melville's 'Eat Labba and drink Creek Water', in *Shape-Shifter*, 148–64.

6. Indeed, this is the title of one of the essays in Lamming's 1960 non-fiction book, *The Pleasures of Exile* (London: Allison & Busby, 1984) in which he discusses the West Indian's historical and cultural relationship to the 'Mother Country'.

7. Sheila Allen, 'Race, Ethnicity and Gender', in Haleh Afshar and Mary Maynard (eds), *The Dynamics of 'Race' and Gender* (London and Bristol, PA: Taylor and Francis, 1994), 100.

8. D'Aguiar, *British Subjects*, 14–15.

9. For example, Jackie Kay's 'Do You Think I'm a Mule', in *A Dangerous Knowing* (London: Sheba, 1984), or 'In My Country', in *Other Lovers* (Newcastle upon Tyne: Bloodaxe, 1993), 24.

10. In 'With Glenda in Brixton Park' (*LTLW* 49), the Caribbean is linked with the freedoms and simplicity of childhood. The poem ends with the moving image of Glenda 'suddenly/ . . . swimming in her own eye/ clotheless/ husbandless/ babyless/ Her dark limbs/ hitting once more/ the blue Caribbean sea'.

11. See for example, Lamming's *The Emigrants* (London: Michael Joseph, 1954), Selvon's *The Lonely Londoners* (Harlow: Longman, 1956) and Salkey's *Escape to an Autumn Pavement* (London: Hutchinson, 1960).

12. Heidi Safia Mirza ed., *Black British Feminism: A Reader* (London and New York: Routledge, 1997), 6. Mirza cites examples from black women soldiers' narratives of the Second World War, the 'writing and campaigns' of Una Marson and more recent texts such as Bryan, Dadzie and Scafe's *The Heart of the Race* (London: Virago, 1985) and Elsye Dodgson's *Motherland: West Indian Women to Britain in the 1950s* (London: Heinemann, 1984).

13. Mirza, *Black British Feminism*, 6..

14. In Donnell and Lawson Welsh (eds), *Routledge Reader in Caribbean Literature*, see for example: Claude McKay's 'My Native Land My Home', 'A Midnight Woman to the Bobby' and 'The Apple-Woman's Complaint' (64–8), Una Marson's 'Quashie Comes To London', 'Kinky Hair Blues' and 'Cinema Eyes' (132–40), Louise Bennett's 'Jamaica Oman', 'Proverbs' and 'Tan a Yuh Yard' (145–9), Christine Craig's 'Elsa's Version' (301), James Berry's 'Lucy's Letter' and 'From Lucy: Holiday Reflections' (380–83) and Jean Binta Breeze's 'Testament' (456–60).

15. Carole Boyce Davies, *Black Women, Writing and Identity: Migrations of the Subject* (London and New York: Routledge, 1994), 110.

16. These include *The Lonely Londoners* (1956), *Ways of Sunlight* (London: Macgibbon & Kee, 1958) and *The Housing Lark* (London: Macgibbon & Kee, 1965).

17. ' "Summer is Hearts" Says Sammy Selvon', *Give Yourself a Hug* (Harmondsworth: Penguin, 1994), 23.

18. This African-derived ritual is also mentioned in 'sunris' (*S* 66).
19. William Shakespeare, *Richard II*, Act II, scene 1.
20. In Caribbean folklore, the Moongazer is a supernatural figure of fearsome size and powers. In *Whole of a Morning Sky*, Gem describes him as 'Standing with his legs astride the road. Tall-tall, with his throw-back head gazing up at the moon. Head almost touching the moon. But only a fool would try to pass between his legs. Only a fool who would want to die would try to slip between them and give him the chance of snapping his legs together, crushing them flatter than a bake. That was the Moongazer for you' (*WMS* 12).
21. Olive Senior also has poems dedicated to Oya and Shango, 'Oya: Goddess of the Wind' and 'Shango: God of Thunder', in *Gardening in the Tropics* (Newcastle upon Tyne: Bloodaxe, 194), 127 and 121–3.
22. Olive Senior makes the same point, that the gods are still alive, in interview with Kwame Dawes (*Talk Yuh Talk: Interviews with Anglophone Caribbean Poets* (Charlottesville and London: University Press of Virginia, 2001), 82). They are also alive in the sense that Shango cults still worship these gods in Trinidad and Tobago, led by Orishas (or Orisha mothers), who are the leaders of the religion.
23. Salman Rushdie, 'Imaginary Homelands', in *Imaginary Homelands: Essays and Criticism 1981–1991* (London: Granta, 1991), 10.
24. The most striking of these is Jamaica Kincaid's *A Small Place* (London: Virago, 1988).
25. The authors of *Key Concepts in Post-Colonial Studies*, Bill Ashcroft, Gareth Griffiths and Helen Tiffin, write on mimicry as an 'increasingly important term in postcolonial theory, because it has come to describe the ambivalent relationship between colonizer and colonized. When colonial discourse encourages the colonized subject to 'mimic' the colonizer, by adopting the colonizer's cultural habits, assumptions, institutions and values, the result is never a simple reproduction of those traits. Rather, the result is a 'blurred copy' of the colonizer that can be quite threatening. This is because mimicry is never very far from mockery, since it can appear to parody whatever it mimics. Mimicry therefore becomes a crack in the certainty of colonial dominance, an uncertainty in its control of the behaviour of the colonized' (London and New York: Routledge, 1998), 139.
26. Derek Walcott, *Epitaph for the Young: A Poem in XII Cantos* (Bridgetown, Barbados: Advocate Co., 1949), This was a self-funded, locally published poem.

27. See also Pauline Melville's 'Eat Labba and Drink Creek Water', 162–4.
28. Fredric Jameson, 'Third World Literature in the Era of Multinational Capitalism', *Social Text*, 15 (1986).
29. Patricia Duncker, *Sisters and Strangers: An Introduction to Contemporary Feminist Fiction* (Oxford and Cambridge, MA: Blackwell, 1992), 236.
30. Gina Wisker, Introduction, *Black Women's Writing* (Basingstoke: Macmillan, 1993), 10. Wisker is specifically referring to Barbara Burford's 'The Landscapes Painted on the Inside of My Skin', *Spare Rib* (June 1987), 37.
31. Grace Nichols and John Agard (eds), *A Caribbean Dozen: Poems from Caribbean Poets* (London: Walker, 1994), 25.
32. See Rushdie's articulation of exactly this point, in his essay 'Imaginary Homelands' which is explored in the discussion of 'cultural hybridity' below.
33. I am indebted to Ruth Robbins for this point.
34. 'Episodically, Nichols details the arson which decimated Georgetown; the general strikes and violence which crippled the economy and brought down Cheddi Jagan's popularly elected people's progressive party (the NLP of the novel); and the Anglo-American role in this destabilisation, which resulted in the ascendancy of Forbes Burnham's party' (O'Callaghan, *Woman Version*, 82).
35. Isabel Hoving discusses the complex (possibly homosexual) identity of Conrad and the ambivalent nature of his relationship with the child Gem in a chapter on Nichols's novel in her recent book, *In Praise of New Travellers* (Stanford: Stanford University Press: 2001), 169–71.
36. Nichols's description of the function of her mother's and the fictional Clara's kitchens as the centres of female community (in 'Home Truths' and *Whole of a Morning Sky* respectively), as well as in her poem 'Between Women' (in Barbara Burford et al., *A Dangerous Knowing: Four Black Women Poets* (London: Sheba, 1985) bear a strikingly resemblance to the women's kitchens described by Barbadian-born African-American writer, Paule Marshall in her essay, 'The Making of a Writer: From the Poets of the Kitchen', *New York Times Book Review*, 9 January 1983; repr. in Henry Louis Gates Jr and Nellie Y. McKay (eds), *The Norton Anthology of African American Literature* (London and New York: W. W. Norton & Co., 1997), 2072–9.

CHAPTER 6. CONCLUSION: BORDER CROSSINGS AND HYBRID FUTURES

1. Françoise Lionnet, *Postcolonial Representations* (Ithaca and London: Cornell University Press, 1995), 27.
2. Kamau Brathwaite, *The Development of Creole Society in Jamaica 1770–1820* (Oxford: Clarendon Press, 1971); Wilson Harris, *Womb of Space: The Cross Cultural Imagination* (Westport, CT: Greenwood Press, 1983); and Derek Walcott, 'The Muse of History', in Orde Coombs (ed.), *Is Massa Day Dead?* (New York: Doubleday/ Anchor Press, 1974), repr. in Donnell and Lawson Welsh, *Routledge Reader in Caribbean Literature*, 356–7.

Select Bibliography

WORKS BY GRACE NICHOLS

Leslyn in London (1978; London: Hodder and Stoughton, 1984).

Trust You, Wriggly (London: Hodder and Stoughton, 1980).

i is a long memoried woman (London: Karnak House, 1983).

Baby Fish and Other Stories (self-published, 1983).

A Wilful Daughter (self-published, 1983).

The Fat Black Woman's Poems (London: Virago, 1984).

The Discovery (London: Macmillan, 1986).

Whole of a Morning Sky (London: Virago, 1986).

Contemporary Literature on Tape: Grace Nichols and Samuel Selvon (London: British Library, National Sound Archive, 1987).

Come On Into My Tropical Garden (London: A & C Black, 1988; reissued London: Young Lions, 1993).

Lazy Thoughts of a Lazy Woman (London: Virago, 1989).

Poetry Jump-Up (Harmondsworth: Penguin, 1989).

No Hickory, No Dickory, No Dock: A Collection of Caribbean Nursery Rhymes with John Agard (London: Viking/ Penguin, 1991).

i is a long memoried woman, radio dramatization, BBC Radio 3 (8 November 1991).

Give Yourself a Hug (London: A & C Black Publishers Ltd, 1994; reissued London: Penguin, 1996).

Sunris (London: Virago, 1996).

Asana and the Animals (London: Walker, 1997).

The Poet-Cat (London: Bloomsbury, 2000).

Paint Me a Poem: New Poems Inspired by Art in the Tate (London: A & C Black, 2004).

From Mouth to Mouth (edited with John Agard).

Starting the Flying Fish (London: Virago 2005).

Everybody Got a Gift (London: A & C Black, 2006).

ANTHOLOGIES THAT INCLUDE POEMS BY
GRACE NICHOLS

Allnutt, Gillian, Fred D'Aguiar, Ken Edwards and Eric Mottram (eds), *The New British Poetry* (London: Paladin, 1988).

Baird, Vanessa (ed.), *Eye to Eye Women* (Oxford: New Internationalist, 1996).

Bax, Martin (ed.), *Ambit* (London: Omnific Ltd, 1982).

Beasley, Paul (ed.), *Hearsay: Performance Poems Plus* (London: Bodley Head, 1994).

Berry, James (ed.), *News for Babylon: The Chatto Book of Westindian-British Poetry* (London: Chatto & Windus, 1984).

Besner, Neil, Deborah Schnitzer and Alden Turner (eds), *Uncommon Wealth: An Anthology of Poetry in English* (Toronto, New York and London: Oxford University Press, 1997).

Bhinda, Madhu (ed.), *Jumping Across Worlds: An Anthology of International Poetry* (UK: NATE, 1994).

Brown, Stewart (ed.), *Caribbean Poetry Now* (London: Edward Arnold, 1984).

Brown, Stewart, Mervyn Morris and Gordon Rohlehr (eds), *Voiceprint: An Anthology of Oral and Related Poetry from the Caribbean* (London: Longman, 1989).

Burford, Barbara, et al., *A Dangerous Knowing: Four Black Women Poets* (London: Sheba, 1985). Poems by Barbara Burford, Jackie Kay, Grace Nichols and Gabriela Pearse.

Burnett, Paula (ed.), *The Penguin Book of Caribbean Verse in English* (Harmondsworth, Middlesex: Penguin, 1986).

Busby, Margaret (ed.), *Daughters of Africa* (London: Vintage, 1992).

Campbell, Elaine, and Pierrette Frickey (eds), *The Whistling Bird: Women Writers of the Caribbean* (Boulder, CO, and London: Lynne Rienner; Jamaica: Ian Randle, 1998).

Cobham, Rhonda, and Merle Collins (eds), *Watchers and Seekers: Creative Writing by Black Women in Britain* (London: Women's Press, 1987).

Dawes, Kwame (ed.), *Wheel and Come Again: An Anthology of Reggae Poetry* (Leeds: Peepal Press, 1998).

Donnell, Alison, and Sarah Lawson Welsh (eds), *The Routledge Reader in Caribbean Literature* (London and New York: Routledge, 1996).

Espinet, Ramabai (ed.), *Creation Fire: A Cafra Anthology of Caribbean Women's Poetry* (Toronto, Canada and Tunapuna, Trinidad: Sister Vision and Cafra, 1990).

France, Linda (ed.), *Sixty Woman Poets* (Newcastle upon Tyne: Bloodaxe, 1993).

Grewal, S., L. Landor and P. Palmer (eds), *Charting the Journey: Writings by Black and Third World Women* (London: Sheba Feminist, 1988).

Healy, Maura (ed.), *Quartet of Poems*. Poems by Grace Nichols, Maya Angelou, Alice Walker and Lorna Goodison (Harlow: Longman,1993).

Horovitz, Michael (ed.), *The Grandchildren of Albion: An Anthology of Voices and Visions of Younger Poets in Britain* (Stroud, Gloucestershire: New Departures, 1992).

Kay, Jackie, Grace Nichols, John Agard, Nick Toczek and Mike Rosen, *Number Parade: Number Poems from 0–100* (London: LDA, 2002).

Kinsman, Judith (ed.), *Six Women Poets* (Oxford: Oxford University Press, 1992).

Linthwaite, Illona (ed.), *Ain't I A Woman!: Poems by Black and White Women* (London: Virago, 1987).

McCarthy, Karen (ed.), *Bittersweet: Contemporary Black Women's Poetry* (London: Women's Press, 1998).

Markham, E. A. (ed.), *Hinterland: Caribbean Poetry from the West Indies and Britain* (Newcastle upon Tyne: Bloodaxe, 1989).

Mordecai, Pamela, and Betty Wilson (eds), *Her True-True Name: An Anthology of Women's Writing from the Caribbean* (Oxford: Heinemann, 1989).

Nichols, Grace (ed.), *Black Poetry* (London: Blackie, 1988; reissued as *Poetry Jump-Up* Harmondsworth: Penguin, 1989).

—— *Can I Buy a Slice of Sky?: Poems from Black, Asian and Amerindian Cultures* (London: Blackie, 1991).

Nichols, Grace, and John Agard (eds), *A Caribbean Dozen: Poems from Caribbean Poets* (London: Walker, 1994).

—— *Under the Moon & Over the Sea: A Collection of Caribbean Poems* (London: Walker, 2002).

—— *From Mouth to Mouth* (London: Walker Books, 2004).

Paskin, Sylvia, Jay Ramsay and Jeremy Silver (eds), *Angels of Fire: An Anthology of Radical Poetry in the '80s* (London: Chatto & Windus, 1986).

Penguin Modern Poets: Jackie Kay, Merle Collins, Grace Nichols, vol. 8 (London: Penguin, 1996).

Procter, James (ed.), *Writing Black Britain: 1948–1998* (Manchester: Manchester University Press, 2000).

Purple and Green: Poems by Women Poets (London: Rivelin Grapheme, 1985).

Rowe, Marsha (ed.), *So Very English* (London: Serpent's Tail, 1991).

Thieme, John (ed.), *The Arnold Anthology of Post-Colonial Literatures* (London: Arnold, 1996).

Wambu, Onyekachi (ed.), *Empire Windrush: Fifty Years of Writing about Black Britain* (London: Victor Gollancz, 1998).

We Couldn't Provide Fish Thumbs. Poems by James Berry, Judith Nicholls, Grace Nichols, Vernon Scannell and Matthew Sweeney (London: Macmillan, 1997).

INTERVIEWS

Butcher, Maggie, 'In Conversation with Grace Nichols', *Wasafiri*, 8 (1988), 17–20.

'Grace Nichols', in Kwame Dawes (ed.), *Talk Yuh Talk: Interviews with Anglophone Caribbean Poets* (Charlottesville and London: University Press of Virginia, 2001), 135–47.

Grace Nichols interviewed on *Woman's Hour*, BBC Radio 4, 1991.

The Poetry of Grace Nichols, programme 3 in the *Poetry Backpack* series for schools, BBC Television 1997.

BIOGRAPHICAL AND CRITICAL STUDIES OF GRACE NICHOLS

Bertram, Vicki, *Kicking Daffodils* (Edinburgh: Edinburgh University Press, 1997).

Bettinger, Elfi, 'Grace Nichols's "Sugar Cane": A Post-Colonial and Feminist Perspective', *Anglistik und Englischunterricht*, 53, 117–27.

Dawes, Kwame, 'Calypso, Carnival and Quiet Concentration', *Poetry London Newsletter*, 1:2 (Autumn 1997), 21–2.

Eagleton, Terry, Review of Grace Nichols, *Poetry Review*, 74: 2 (1984).

France, Linda, 'High Days and Holidays' (review of *Penguin Modern Poets: Jackie Kay, Merle Collins, Grace Nichols*, vol. 8, and Grace Nichols's *Sunris*), *Poetry Review*, 86:4, Winter 1996–7, 74–5.

Fraser, Peter, 'i is a long memoried woman', in Lauretta Ngcobo (ed.), *Let It Be Told: Black Women Writers in Britain*, (London: Virago, 1988), 104–5.

Gohrisch, Jana, 'Gender and Hybridity in Contemporary Caribbean Poetry', in Raimund Borgmeier, Herbert Grabes and Andreas H. Jucker (eds), *Anglistentag 1997 Giessen: Proceedings* (Trier: WVT, 1998), 139–56.

Griffin, Gabriele, 'Writing the Body: Reading Joan Riley, Grace Nichols and Ntozake Shange', in Gina Wisker (ed.), *Black Women's Writing*, (Basingstoke: Macmillan Press, 1993), 19–42.

Montefiore, Jan, *Feminism and Poetry: Language, Experience, Identity in Women's Writing* (London: Pandora, 1987).

Nichols, Grace, 'Grace Nichols', in Lauretta Ngcobo (ed.), *Let It Be Told: Black Women Writers in Britain*, (London: Virago, 1988), 95–104.

—— 'Home Truths', in E. A. Markham (ed.), *Hinterland: Caribbean Poetry from the West Indies and Britain* (Newcastle upon Tyne: Bloodaxe, 1989), 296–8.

—— 'The Battle with Language', in Selwyn R. Cudjoe (ed.), *Caribbean Women Writers: Essays from the First International Conference* (Wellesley, MA: Calaloux, 1990), 283–9.

—— 'The poetry I feel closest to', in W. N. Herbert amd Matthew Hollis (eds) *Strong Words: Modern Poets on Modern Poetry*, (Newcastle upon Tyne: Bloodaxe, 2000), 211–12.

Papaleonida, Paraskevi, ' "holding my beads in my hand": Dialogue, Synthesis and Power in the Poetry of Jackie Kay and Grace Nichols', in Vicki Bertram (ed.), *Kicking Daffodils: Twentieth-Century Women Poets* (Edinburgh: Edinburgh University Press, 1997), 125–39.

Pratt, Akua, review of *i is a long memoried woman*, *Frontline*, Caribbean Cultural International Karnak House, 1983.

Shaw, Marion, review of Grace Nichols, *Poetry Review*, 78: 3 (1988).

Webhofer, Gudrun, *'Identity' in the Poetry of Grace Nichols and Lorna Goodison* (Lewiston, NY: Edwin Mellen Press, 1996).

Woodcock, Bruce, 'Long Memoried Women: Caribbean Women Poets' in Gina Wisker (ed.), *Black Women's Writing* (Basingstoke: Macmillan Press, 1993), 55–77.

BACKGROUND READING

Berry, James, Introduction, *Bluefoot Traveller: An Anthology of West Indian Poets in Britain* (London: Limehouse Publications: 1976).

—— Introduction, *Bluefoot Traveller*, 2nd edn (Walton-on-Thames: Thomas Nelson & Sons, 1981).

Brah, Avtar, *Cartographies of Diaspora: Contesting Identities* (London and New York: Routledge, 1996). An ambitious, theoretically informed intervention into a range of contemporary debates concerning difference and diversity. Useful for its discussion of the dynamics of diaspora, border crossings and the politics of location. Chapter 8 is particularly useful in this respect.

Brathwaite, Kamau, *History of the Voice* (London: New Beacon, 1984). Essential reading on the language politics of the Caribbean.

Bryan, Beverley, Stella Dadzie and Suzanne Scafe, *The Heart of the Race: Black Women's Lives in Britain* (London: Virago, 1985). Still a classic nearly twenty years on. Multi-disciplinary in focus. See chapter 5 on culture and identity.

Conde, Mary and Thorunn Lonsdale (eds), *Caribbean Women Writers: Fiction in English* (London: Macmillan, 1999). Essays on a range of women writers, including fellow Guyanese Pauline Melville plus a small number of contributions by practising writers.

Cudjoe, Selwyn R. (ed.), *Caribbean Women Writers: Essays from the First International Conference* (Wellesley, MA: Calaloux, 1990). Contains a variety of useful contextual materials for a reading of Nichols's work, as well as pieces by practising writers. Nichols's contribution, 'The Battle with Language' first appeared as 'Grace Nichols' in Lauretta Ngcobo (ed.), *Let It Be Told* (London: Virago, 1988).

Dabydeen, David, and Nana Wilson-Tagoe, *A Reader's Guide to West Indian and Black British Literature* (London: Hansib, 1988; rev. edn 1997). Brief but very accessible overview of the historical background, cultural contexts and thematic concerns of the literature.

Davies, Carole Boyce, *Black Women Writing and Identity: Migrations of the Subject* (London and New York: Routledge, 1994). A lively and wide-ranging introduction to a range of issues pertinent to a reading of Nichols's work. The introductory chapter on 'Migratory Subjectivities' and the last section of chapter 4 (pp. 96–111), which focuses on black British women writers, are particularly useful

Davies, Carole Boyce and Elaine Savory Fido (eds), *Out of the Kumbla: Caribbean Women and Literature* (Trenton, NJ: Africa World Press, 1990). A more theorized set of essays than those in Cudjoe's, *Caribbean Women Writers*. Pan-Caribbean in focus, with extensive bibliographic information.

Dawes, Kwame (ed.), *Talk Yuh Talk: Interviews with Anglophone Caribbean Poets* (Charlottesville and London: University Press of Virginia, 2001). Besides including a recent and highly illuminating interview with Nichols, *Talk Yuh Talk* provides a good introduction to both established and newer voices from the Caribbean.

De Caires Narain, Denise, *Contemporary Caribbean Women's Poetry: Making Style* (London and New York: Routledge, 2002). Illuminating and eminently readable introduction to the subject. Examines women poets' relationship to literary tradition in the Caribbean plus language politics, performance aesthetic and impact of gender on genre. Chapter 4 provides useful reading of Nichols's work alongside that of Lorna Goodison, Mahadai Das and Marlene Nourbese Philip.

Donnell, Alison, and Sarah Lawson Welsh (eds), *The Routledge Reader in Caribbean Literature* (London and New York: Routledge, 1996). Collects together a wide range of primary and secondary resources which can be difficult to access separately. Usefully provides historical and cultural introductions to particular decades/periods as well as plotting the main developments and concerns of Anglophone Caribbean literature.

Duncker, Patricia, *Sisters and Strangers: An Introduction to Contemporary Feminist Fiction* (Oxford: Blackwell, 1992), 210–9. Chapter 7, 'Writing Against Racism', focuses on black British women's writing, including work by Nichols.

Lawson Welsh, Sarah, 'Critical Myopia and Black British Literature: Reassessing the Literary Contribution of the Post-Windrush Generation(s)', *Kunapipi*, 20:1, 132–42. A special Windrush issue commemorating fifty years of West Indian presence in Britain, which provides useful contextual materials for the study of Nichols in a black British literary framework.

—— '(Un)belonging Citizens, Unmapped Territory: Black Immigration and British Identity in the Post-1945 Period', in Stuart Murray (ed.), *Not On Any Map: Essays on Postcoloniality and Cultural Nationalism* (Exeter: Exeter University Press, 1997), 43–66. Looks at issues of citizenship and cultural nationalism in a British context, with a special focus on black British cultural praxis. Includes close readings of two poems by black British poets, Fred D'Aguiar and Merle Collins.

McLaughlin, Andrée Nicola, 'Black Women, Identity, and the Quest for Humanhood and Wholeness: Wild Women in the Whirlwind', in Joanna M. Braxton and Andree Nicola McLaughlin (eds), *Wild Women in the Whirlwind: Afra-American Culture and the Contemporary Literary Renaissance* (London: Serpents Tail, 1990), 147–80. Includes a short section on black British writers (pp. 163–7), discussed within a wider diasporic context.

Mirza, Heidi Safia (ed.), *Black British Feminisms: A Reader* (London and New York: Routledge, 1997). Multidisciplinary in focus. General background reading.

Nasta, Susheila (ed.), *Motherlands: Black Women's Writing from Africa, the Caribbean and South Asia* (London: Women's Press, 1991). Worth reading for the introduction alone. Includes a series of essays on different aspects of mothers, mothering and motherlands within a range of feminist and postcolonial contexts.

—— 'Beyond the Millennium: Black Women's Writing', *Women: A Cultural Review*, 11:1/2 (2000), 71–6. Good on the critical neglect of black women's writing in Britain.

Newson, A. S., and L. Strong-Leek (eds), *Winds of Change: The Transforming Voices of Caribbean Women Writers and Scholars* (New York: Peter Lang, 1998). An incisive and enabling series of essays

ISBN 0820437158

142

on aspects of the study of Caribbean women's writing. Strong on language politics. Also includes a provocative essay by L. Paravisni-Gebert on 'The Pitfalls of Theorising Caribbean Women's Writing', 161–8.

Ngcobo, Lauretta (ed.), *Let It Be Told: Black Women Writers in Britain* (London: Virago, 1988). Still a key resource book for anyone interested in black women's writing in Britain. Includes an extensive and useful introduction plus ten essays by black women writers, including Nichols.

O'Callaghan, Evelyn, *Woman Version: Theoretical Approaches to West Indian Fiction by Women* (London: Macmillan, 1993). Although this study does not focus on black British women writers *per se*, useful for its innovative theoretical approach to and readings of a range of Caribbean women's writing. Chapter 5 includes substantial attention to *Whole of a Morning Sky*.

Rushdie, Salman, *Imaginary Homelands: Essays and Criticism 1981–1991* (London: Granta, 1991). The title essay from this collection is most pertinent to a reading Nichols's work. Beyond this, readers may find the first five sections useful.

Walder, Dennis (ed.), *Post-colonial Literatures in English* (Oxford: Blackwell, 1998). Chapter 6 of this very accessible introduction to the field focuses on Caribbean and black British poetry and includes discussion of Nichols's poetry alongside that of Linton Kwesi Johnson and James Berry in the 'New Voices, New Memories' section, 140–48.

Williams, Patrick, 'Difficult Subjects: Black British Women's Poetry', in David Murray (ed.), *Literary Theory and Poetry: Extending the Canon* (London: Batsford, 1989), 108–26. An early but useful essay on the subject. Includes discussion of *i is*.

Wisker, Gina (ed.), *Black Women's Writing* (Basingstoke: Macmillan Press, 1993). Chapters 2, 3 and 4 provide productively diverse readings of black women's writing in Britain and the Caribbean, as well as reflecting on some of the wider issues relating to the publishing and teaching of such texts. Very useful introduction but no general bibliography is included.

—— *Post-Colonial and African-American Women's Writing* (Basingstoke: Macmillan, 2000). Wisker's latest study is wider in scope than *Black Women's Writing* but less in-depth in its analysis. However, it usefully includes a separate chapter on black British women's writing (ch. 12, pp. 273–300), besides that on Caribbean women's writing (ch. 5, pp. 93–129). Discussion of Nichols's work appears in both chapters.

143

Young, Lola, 'What is Black British Feminism?', *Women: A Cultural Review*, 11:1/2 (2000), 45–59. Young at her polemical and thought-provoking best. Discusses how the terms 'black' and 'feminism' 'might work effectively together' in contemporary Britain, in ways which usefully update the debates of the 1980s.

Index

Printed in the United Kingdom
by Lightning Source UK Ltd.
125431UK00002BA/1-57/A